FEARLESS

My Life's Destiny

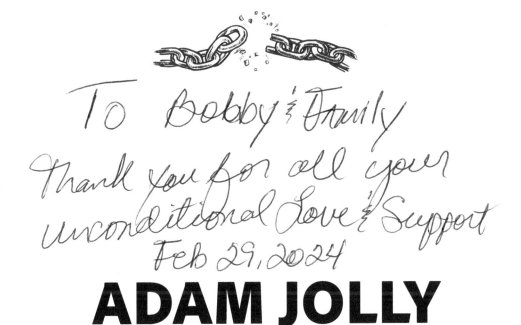

To Bobby & Family
Thank you for all your
unconditional Love & Support
Feb 29, 2024

ADAM JOLLY

DVP
publishing

Don't Vacuum Publishing
publishing

Published by
DP Diversified
a division of DocUmeant Publishing
244 5th Avenue, Suite G-200
NY, NY 10001
Phone: 6462334366

http://www.DocUmeantPublishing.com

For permission contact the publisher at:
publisher@DocUmeantPublishing.com

Disclaimer: I have tried to recreate events, locales and conversations from my memories of them. In order to maintain their anonymity in some instances I have changed the names of individuals and places, I may have changed some identifying characteristics and details such as physical properties, occupations and places of residence.

All scripture quotations are taken from The New King James Version / Thomas Nelson Publishers, Nashville : Thomas Nelson Publishers., Copyright 1982. Used by permission. All rights reserved.

Editor: Philip S. Marks

Cover Design and Layout: Ginger Marks, DocUmeantDesigns.com

Library of Congress Cataloging-in-Publication Data

Names: Jolly, Adam, 1964- author.
Title: Fearless : my life's destiny / Adam Jolly.
Other titles: My life's destiny
Description: New York, NY : DP Diversified, [2024] | Includes
   bibliographical references.
Identifiers: LCCN 2024003387 | ISBN 9781957832272 (pbk) | ISBN
   9781957832289 (digital)
Subjects: LCSH: Jolly, Adam, 1964- | African Americans--Florida--Biography.
   | African American prisoners--Florida--Biography. | African American
   clergy--Florida--Biography. | Prisoners--Florida--Biography. |
   Clergy--Florida--Biography. | Florida--Biography.
Classification: LCC F316.23.J65 A3 2024 | DDC 975.900496/0730092
   [B]--dc23/eng/20240215
LC record available at https://lccn.loc.gov/2024003387

Dedication

THIS BOOK IS dedicated to my great-grandparents, Mr. and Mrs. Henry and Jennie Griffin, who gave me unconditional love, attention, and the affection I needed. Because of their dedicated support, they will forever be my heroes and serve as my inspiration.

To my beloved, beautiful children Yashekia, Amanda (deceased), Candee, Jeremiah, Adam, Raven, Turquoise, and Leryia thank you for all your affection, the hugs, kisses, letters, cards, pictures, and the times we exchanged the words "I Love You."

To the men in the wrong army, sense the urgency to change from the inside out and come into God's kingdom with your hands up to live in the newness of life.

To the brothers and sisters who have been trying to fill that void in your souls but have been unsuccessful, the answer is in this book. It was written just for you. It was destined to land in your hands to bless you.

Contents

Acknowledgments

THERE ARE SO many people who were a part of who I was and who I am today that deserve to be recognized.

First and foremost, to my wife, Ingrid Queen-Jolly, thank you for being the wind beneath my wings and the joy of my life.

To the educators who spoke into my life and saw the best in me when I didn't see it myself; Mrs. Gloria McHardy, my 4th-grade teacher, Mr. Charles Anderson, P.E. Coach, and Mr. Don Wallen, Asst. Principal, and legendary basketball coach.

To the late Pastor Henry Lewis and the mothers of Macedonia church prayed for me through, Mrs. Willie Mae Johnson, Mrs. Hattie Green, Mrs. Atline Cooper, Mrs. Janie Mae, and Mrs. Williams.

To the different volunteer prison ministries that came into Madison, Cross City, Desoto, and Martin Correctional Institutions who ministered to me.

To the faithful sold-out brethren who helped groom me in the faith. Woodrow Jackson, Ernest Atterbury, Dereck Thompson, David Jones, Bruce Downey, Calvin Jackson, Jeffrey Banks, Marcus Julien, James Brown, James Sanders, Enrique Myers, and Daniel Williams.

Finally, to my spiritual parents, Bishop Gerald and Rev. Novlet Green, and the late Bishop Derrick W. Hutchins.

Foreword

ONCE A THUG, now a hug, Adam Jolly has lived a life that has come full circle. Raised in a drug infested neighborhood and in a family that sold drugs from their home, Adam didn't have much access to a lawful lifestyle. Discipline came in the form of a backhand smack. Adam became desensitized to the justice system early in his life when he visited his uncles and brothers in prison and when he watched members of his community buying drugs from his immediate family. As a young teen he learned how to make money selling drugs to schoolmates. Adam was a ready-made, stamped out, product of his environment. The attraction to the criminal lifestyle was natural. It seemed there wasn't any other option for him than to continue the lifestyle he had been raised in.

While growing up, Adam's hustle became selling drugs, working the streets, committing armed robberies, and trying to become better at his game. Arrest and incarceration were natural outcomes, a way of life, an expected path on his life's journey. It is very sad to think about, but true. In the hood, prison time gives you credentials, 'creds,' on the street.

Incarcerated four times, his last sentence was for 50 years. The court system and law enforcement didn't want him outside ever again. He was too much to handle. Adam was at war with his community and God and needed to be put away for good. As a former Special Agent for the Federal Bureau of Investigation commented, he was the kind of guy I felt should be separated from society.

But here is the good news. While serving that lengthy sentence, he started walking a new path. Unhappy and miserable with his past, he knew he needed a spiritual change, a rebirth, in military terms, a real about face. So, on his knees, in his cell with his Bible falling open to Romans 10:9, Adam received Christ. That verse has become his guiding light. After that life-changing experience there was no turning back. After serving 22 years and representing himself on an illegal sentence, he was granted immediate release and placed on probation for eight years.

Early on in this whole process, Adam set his goals for his future. First of all, after his release, he earned his Masters degree in Christian counseling, then his Doctorate in Divinity and theology. He became a business owner and was ordained as a minister. He serves his local community by pastoring a church and helping newly released men and women transition back into society. He began the Bread From Heaven Ministries in Stuart, Florida, to serve the less fortunate and is presently working for the Jack Brewer Foundation as a Program Coordinator.

The war between Adam and God has been over for some time now. Adam won the peace offered in Luke 2:14 — the peace upon men on whom Christ's favor rests.

Adam and I have been working together in the prison system for the past three years. Being a former federal law enforcement officer and a man of faith, I was very pleased to be introduced to a man who is on fire for God and His

Son. When I was introduced to him, I knew Adam had done 28 years in prison for some major offenses and was unsure what to expect. What I found was a man in the midst of his destiny. I am honored to be his friend.

I recommend this book to those who enjoy reading of the success of real people who had tough beginnings but overcame their situations by changing their paths and creating new futures for themselves and others.

Kenneth C. McKenzie

One

Dropped Off at Ma Jennie's House

I WAS BORN a handsome little fellow on September 11, 1964, at Glades General Hospital, Belle Glade, Florida. My father, Wenzel Jolly, was a native of Nassau, Bahamas, and my mother, Jennie Mae (*Glover*) Jolly was a beautiful muck-stepping girl from Belle Glade who my father had to have.[1] For whatever reason, my parents gave me over to my great-grandparents, Henry Griffin (*Mr. Henry*) and Jennie Griffin (*Ma Jennie, a/k/a Mama*) to be raised on Tarpon Ave., East Stuart, Florida, where they lived.

Ma Jennie was born November 15, 1899, on Reynolds Plantation, Edgefield County, South Carolina. She was the oldest daughter of James Ware. She had two sisters and two brothers. Ma Jennie's friends called her "Jennie Slim" because she was 6-foot 3-inches tall and was attractive physically. She was also known as a fighter among her siblings and friends in their neighborhood. Ma Jennie married her first husband, Pastor Will Dawson and birthed her only child, Viola Glover. Later, Ma Jennie moved to Augusta, Georgia and worked at the Riverside Cotton Mill until she retired and moved to Stuart, Florida in 1956.

Before she moved to Florida, she met and married Henry Griffin. Mr. Henry was a respectable hard-working man. In his early years, he wanted to become a professional boxer until his brother died while boxing in the ring. It was after his mother convinced him not to box that he met and married Ma Jennie and they moved to Florida.

I was dropped off at Ma Jennie's house at a very young age, just before I started kindergarten. In Ma Jennie's house church attendance was mandatory every Sunday at Macedonia Baptist Church. She raised a total of twelve of us. That is, my two brothers and me, plus seven uncles and one aunt. Because I was the youngest Ma Jennie spent more time with me than the others and taught me a lot. I can still hear her prayers today unto the Lord for her boys—"LORD, please don't let the Devil kill my boys."

As a little boy, I always heard around the neighborhood that Ma Jennie and her boys were gangsters. That statement alone inflamed my ego for the next 32 years, trying to live up to others' expectations of what they thought a gangster should be. Also, being raised on Tarpon Ave., a high-crime and drug-infested neighborhood, affected my mindset and shaped my life concept of living a life of crime with no serious regard to the consequences.

Though I learned how to play baseball better than any kid my age from my Uncle Jerry O'Bryant (O.B.) and my middle school physical education (P.E.) coach, Charles Anderson, trouble and a street life of crime already had its hooks in me.

My great-grandfather nicknamed me "Turk." In fact, Mr. Henry also nicknamed my oldest brother Arthur Glover, "Peas;" my other brother Lincoln Jolly, "Duck" and my youngest uncle Ralph Glover, "Bean." Can you imagine the menu and line up at dinner call? By the way, Mr. Henry's nickname in the neighborhood was "Mr. Valley." He was an ex-prizefighter in South Carolina who was a big, tough Black man with a booming voice and large, rough hands.

If child abuse laws had been in effect during the late sixties and early seventies, Ma Jennie and Mr. Henry would have been doing some serious time. All the neighborhood kids on Tarpon loved to hear Mr. Henry's booming voice during role call at dinnertime—"Turk (*me*), Duck, Bean, and Peas!" The other kids loved teasing us as we responded by going home for dinner.

Ma Jennie and Mr. Henry had a small chicken and pigeon farm in their backyard. They also had collard and turnip greens growing in a nice garden in the side yard. This is why it was easy for Mr. Henry to nickname Ma Jennie's boys after some animals and vegetables that were not in their pen or garden.

For certain meals, guess who had to ring and pop the chicken and or pigeons' necks? Turk (*me*), Duck, Bean, or Peas! Whenever fresh eggs were laid, guess who had to fight with the rooster (*king of the chicken pen*) to fetch the eggs from the hens' nests? Turk, Duck, Bean, or Peas! When it was time for the greens to be pulled up or the chicken pen to be cleaned up, guess who had to do it? You probably know who by now.

The experience and degree I received from the school of Ma Jennie and

Mr. Henry prepared me for my first real job with the local neighborhood contractor,

Mr. Tom Allen, who owned a landscaping and sod business. He was the man who provided work for every young boy, teenager, and or adult who needed work in our local East Stuart neighborhood. Duck, Bean, Peas, David Lee (*one of my uncles*), and I all worked for Mr. Allen.

In 1975 when I was 11, we worked full time in the summer and only on weekends during the school year. We laid grass throughout the entire Martin County area from Hobe Sound, Palm City, and Stuart, to Jensen Beach.

Mr. Henry and Ma Jennie decided that we had to start assuming more responsibility by giving them 20-percent of our earnings to help pay bills and life insurance. This brought to mind an incident that happened one day while coming home from school. I noticed an unusual crowd outside our house. As I got closer to the house, I started to hear different people talking about how Ma Jennie broke the insurance man's arm. Her version to me was that while she was putting on her bra, homeboy had the nerve to walk in on her in her bedroom to collect his insurance money. Ma Jennie said, "He must have lost his White mind (*he was a White man*)." The only thing he collected that day was a broken arm.

Also, when I was eleven, Ma Jennie became my hero. Several months after the insurance man incident her only son Irvin got slick out his mouth with my hero concerning his daughter Kim. Everybody in the house knew that meant trouble and something was about to pop off quickly that was going to inflict some fierce pain. Ma Jennie was babysitting Irvin's oldest daughter and Irvin sent for her to come home. When she didn't come home, he showed up to get her and Ma Jennie refused to let her go home with him. When Irvin demanded that Ma Jennie let his daughter leave with him, that's when this first-round knockout happened. It was either going to be a Muhammad Ali swift knock-out punch or a Larry Holmes' stiff jab with a Mike Tyson right cross. Ma Jennie hit Irvin with a forceful right back-hand blow to his face that drew blood from his nose and tears from his eyes. Irvin was about 32 years old and he knew without a doubt that any attempt to raise his hand to Ma Jennie would result in a brutal beat down by Mr. Henry, who was waiting in the corner like the prize fighter he was, to finish off his opponent. With that blow, Ma Jennie had some choice words for Irvin as he stumbled out the front porch door.

Endnotes

I   Belle Glade is referred to as "The Muck" because of its rich soil.

Two

David Lee and Mr. Henry, Rest On in Peace

ON THE FOURTH of July 1970, an unfortunate tragedy happened in our family that I will never forget. Most of the Black communities would gather at the Jensen Beach Causeway on weekends and holidays. That year, someone standing in the crowd out on the pier said he would give twenty dollars to whoever wasn't afraid to jump into the water to get a soda can he was about to throw out there. Upon that challenge, the crowd and I watched my Uncle David swan dive beautifully like Tarzan into the water. To everyone's surprise Uncle David's best friend Steve, who couldn't swim, jumped in behind him.

What was a beautiful afternoon suddenly turned for the worse as the moment froze everyone in time. I was an eyewitness to a cheerful and proud moment that turned into a sad and tragic accident. After my Uncle David swam toward and grabbed the can he turned around and was surprised to see someone gasping for air desperately just a few feet away. Not knowing that it was his best friend Steve who was drowning, Uncle David reached out to help him and they both went underwater. Nearly several hundred spectators saw them drown. Fear and anger gripped my heart; people around me began to scream and cry as we all ran off the pier toward the shore. As people shouted for help, for someone to do something, experienced divers and swimmers entered the water to search for Uncle David and Steve.

After about an hour, Steve was recovered from the water. As his lifeless body was pulled out of the water, Steve showed no signs that he was breathing. Immediately the paramedics performed CPR on him which didn't seem to work. I was staring at the body of a dead man for the first time in my young life. Mr. Henry had nicknamed Steve "Ghuna" because he was a unique family friend who Ma Jennie helped raise as her own child. His sisters, Norma, Kim, and Jazz used to call me "Turkey Red" because I had red hair. As I reflected on how Steve used to tell funny jokes and tickle me causing me to laugh uncontrollably, reality began to settle in on my mind and it really hit me that Steve was dead. Then, all of a sudden, a miracle happened right before me and everyone else who was standing nearby, Steve's legs began to move and his upper body began shaking as he started throwing up water and seaweed. The Jaws of Death lost their grip on Steve's soul as the Breath of Life jump-started his heart and miraculously revived his inner being. We all rejoiced in the moment that Steve was alive and that he was going to make it but the cold, dark fact was that Uncle David's body was still under water for over an hour.

Lorenzo Robinson, a man from our neighborhood who helped recover Steve's body, returned to help search for Uncle David's body. As the sun went down, everyone except the search and rescue team went home. Several hours later they found and recovered Uncle David's body. His funeral was held a week later at Macedonia Baptist Church, an event I will never forget.

Uncle David had passed away at such an early age. He was the most humble and brightest out of all of Ma Jennie's boys. He was always quiet and soft spoken with a warm, genuine smile. Ma Jennie's only daughter, Viola Glover, was Uncle David's mother and my grandmother. Viola stayed in Belle Glade and allowed Ma Jennie to raise all six of her sons and one of her five daughters in East Stuart. Viola birthed her sons, but we were all Ma Jennie's boys.

Life somehow went on as though this unfortunate situation never happened. Just when things seemed to be getting back to normal Mr. Henry's (*my great-grand-father*) health began to fail him and he became very ill. The hospital and doctors gave up on him and sent him home with an assigned nurse to care for him until he passed away.

Mr. Henry's deteriorating health affected everyone in the house. His bed claimed his strength as his massive body withered. His booming voice became a whisper, and his steps grew shorter and shorter as he went back and forth to the restroom.

One day at school I received the news that Mr. Henry had passed away at home. As I walked home from school, I reflected on my fond memories of Mr. Henry. He worked for the City of Stuart Garbage and Transportation Department for many years. Mr. Henry and Ma Jennie always made sure that they provided the necessities we needed. In fact, they also made sure that my brothers and I visited our parents every other weekend on The Muck in Belle Glade. That was always fun, and an adventure for me because The Muck is a unique place. The Muck in Belle Glade is home to some of the richest soil in the world where sugarcane and corn is cultivated. Her soil is her fortune. There is a true saying— "The Muck in Belle Glade and Pahokee has produced more NFL players per capita than any other city in America."

When I was a shorty (*young child*), Mr. Henry used to ride me around East Stuart on his three-wheeled bike. It gave him a great sense of pride and joy to show off his youngest great-grandson to his close friends and buddies. Riding around with Mr. Henry at a young age exposed me to every trap and area where the life of crime and hustling was going down in East Stuart.

Some of those traps and areas included Mr. Blue's Pool Hall, Mr. Teddy and Big Jack's Number and Gambling Houses, an area where adults played checkers under the trees behind the Dixie Bar, Club 19, the Cherokee Motel, and Mrs. Annie's Bar. Mr. Henry used to take me by Mrs. Cynthia's Barber Shop to get haircuts. Afterward I would get the opportunity to choose from which local store to buy some cookies and candy, whether it was Mr. Dunns', George Taylor's, Mr. Luther Ball's, or Mrs. Magalen and Mr. Shorty's Place. Mr. Shorty's Place was my favorite because that's where a lot of action took place such as gambling, checkers, dominoes, prostitution, and drugs. Often, fights would break out in which someone would be stabbed or shot.

Though Mr. Henry never verbally expressed his love to me, my brothers, uncles, or aunts, his consistent actions spoke volumes of his unconditional love for us all. However, no one wanted to see or encounter his disciplinary side. His warnings were simple, brief, and direct. Whenever his warnings weren't adhered to or taken seriously for being disobedient, disrespectful, or crossing a certain line, his disciplinary actions were swift and painful. This meant it only took two or three landed punches anywhere on the body and it was over. Mr. Henry didn't play.

Early in the year the family and friends celebrated Mr. Henry and Ma Jennies' last anniversary together at O.T.'s Nightclub on Monterey Road. Mr. Henry was the backbone of the family and Ma Jennie was the glue that kept it together. My reflection of Mr. Henry Griffin had come full circle, I found myself standing before his open casket in Macedonia Baptist Church, honoring him in his passing. Viewing his body, seeing his face for the very last time with tears running down my face, I could still hear his deep, booming voice for our dinner role call in my mind—"Turk, Duck, Bean, and Peas."

Three

The Backbone with the Equalizers

LIFE FOR ME began to take on a whole new meaning from that day forward. At a family gathering it was obvious that Ma Jennie was now the backbone of the family. She was the glue that was going to keep the family together. Jimmy Glover (*Ski-Bo*), my second oldest uncle, became the disciplinarian and the enforcer in the family whenever anyone disrespected or crossed the line with Ma Jennie.

Ski-Bo was a Vietnam Veteran who was trained to kill and to hurt people, so homeboy wasn't the one to play with—I think you get the picture. In fact, Ski-Bo was the only male in our family who was living a clean, moral, and decent non-criminal life. Gradually however, the opposite lifestyle that the two of my other uncles were living began to appeal more to me than I could resist.

My oldest uncle, O.B., was a flamboyant dresser and real-life throwback playboy, drug pusher, and a very talented and gifted singer. Charles Glover (*Mickey*), my third oldest uncle, also served in the Vietnam War. The same day Mickey returned home from Vietnam, he upped a gun threatening to kill James Johnson about his own wife, Debra Johnson. He didn't come home with a full deck upstairs, but he knew what he wanted. Mickey was always a smooth-talking ladies' man who also came home a junkie and dope pusher.

Being the youngest in the house, Mama took notice that I was beginning to grow up too fast. Her way of keeping a close eye on me, to slow me down, was to pick me out often to wash the dishes, clean the yard or take the clothes off the line in the backyard. I thought she was psychic because she would tell me things that came to pass.

One day when I was helping her take the clothes off the line, she told me that when I grew older I would have a lot of children and I better take care of every one of them the best I knew how. I looked up at her as if to say *What in the world is she talking about?* because I didn't have a clue at the age of eleven.

At the beginning of every school year, our birthdays, and at Christmastime

Ma Jennie took Turk, Duck, Bean, and Peas to JCPenny for new clothes. It was Ma Jennie who took us to the Western Auto Store for bikes, B.B. guns and toys. It was Ma Jennie who took us to the doctor, dentist, or Health Department when necessary. Sometimes she would be our doctor and patch us up with old Black Folk remedies. One time when I had a nasty cut on my arm from a piece of broken glass, she told me to go on the back porch and bring her some spider webs to miraculously heal the cut. We lived in a three-bedroom wooden house that had a screened-in front porch, so I knew where the spiders hung out. Then she would go into the yard and get a limb off of an aloe plant, break it in half, wipe some of the slimy aloe juice on the cut and tape up my arm with the spider web. Within two weeks you couldn't tell that I had been cut. I didn't know that my great-grandmother was a doctor!

On another occasion, one day after school, Mr. Kenny's German Shepard bit me on my left hip. Ma Jennie basically used the same aloe remedy with a few other ingredients that healed me up. The dog bite episode was just like a scene out of the Tom and Jerry cartoon show. I used to walk past Mr. Kenny's apartment behind the Cherokee Motel on purpose just to agitate the dog. He used to go ballistic, barking and growling while trying to get me. It was fun and a great laugh for me. I wasn't scared of this big German Shepard because I knew that he was limited as to how far he could go. He was tethered with a chain around his neck. So, I knew I could only go up so far near a landmark. One day for some reason I went beyond the landmark, I guess you know what happened to me. It was my first out-of-body experience. Just like a scene on the Tom and Jerry show.

Once a month Mama required us to drink a few swigs of castor oil. I thought she was going too far with these remedies. The purpose of drinking castor oil was for bowel movements, among other things. Since Duck, Bean, and Peas had to drink the castor oil, guess who else had to drink it? —Turk.

It came to pass that I became rebellious, refusing to drink castor oil and refusing to clean chitlins because I hated the way it both tasted and smelled. My behavior brought out the wrath and disciplinary side of Ma Jennie. She would literally tell me to go outside to get a limb off the tree so she could beat me with it. Being my rebellious self, I would get one of the smallest limbs I saw. This, of course, would make Ma Jennie angrier at me. If she was really upset with me, she would rush outside to get the biggest limb she saw. I used to pretend dramatically by shedding tears and slobbering from my mouth, all before the first lick even landed. My famous line was "Mama I am sorry; I am not going to do it anymore !" The problem at this point was that I was 11 years old and that line wasn't working for me anymore. The beatings wouldn't stop until she was satisfied or saw some blood. I had grown numb to the beatings, so it was like my "fix" for the week.

On other occasions when I was disobedient or being "mannish" as she would often tell me, Mama would grab the first object she got her hands on to beat me with. She did the same thing with my brothers. Ma Jennie had an arsenal of "equalizers" to choose from such as an extension cord, an ironing cord, a clothes hanger, a water hose, a fan belt, and even a bull whip. Several times when I thought I wasn't going to get a beating for things I knew warranted beatings, Mama gave me some unpleasant, memorable bath tub butt naked beatings. Mama would quietly ease into the bathroom with the extension cord or other such equalizer in her hand and all of a sudden just like in a Dracula horror film, Mama would snatch the shower curtain to the side and let my naked, wet, soapy flesh have it. I felt like a fish trapped in a bowl trying to get somewhere. The thing that sort of confused me and really made me mad was the fact that after the beatings she would often tell me that she loved me and then she would hug and kiss my jaw. Her kisses sometimes would leave a smear and the smell of CC Snuff (*chewing tobacco*) on my face. What could I say or do? This was Ma Jennie who had seen and raised four generations. She dipped that

CC Snuff like baseball players dipped Red Man Tobacco. Though her hugs and kisses were a genuine comfort to my soul, those stinging licks and welts from the extension cord had a very uncomfortable lasting effect on my body.

There were three reasons why I would get mandatory bedroom beatings. First, for not taking a bath before going to bed; second, for not cleaning the bathtub after bathing and third, for putting sausages or hot dogs in a pot on the stove on high heat and then dozing off to sleep while they burned, filling the house with smoke. The following are two examples of repercussions for not bathing before bed and not cleaning the bathtub. Mama would wait purposely until I was into my deepest sleep, then she would enter the room like the Terminator with an equalizer in her hand. Since my brother Duck and I shared the same bed, he would get surprised by the first few stinging licks before Ma Jennie got to her intended target. Duck and I would both wake up dazedly to the rapid fire of direct licks on every part of our respective bodies. Waking up to this familiar trauma scene one time too many, I began using Duck as a human shield. When the licks started I would immediately grab and use my human shield to avoid getting hit as we both hollered. When Mama separated us to zero in on me, she would proceed to beat the brakes off me while saying things like "didn't I tell you . . . I am tired of talking to you . . . put your hands down . . . don't you run from me."

The third reason for repercussions resulted from a very bad habit I engaged in after coming home very hungry late at night while everyone else was asleep. I would boil a few sausages or hot dogs for several minutes and would be satisfied as soon as I ate them. Afterward, however, I would often find myself waking up under Ma Jennie's rounds of serious direct licks without Duck, my human shield. Because my brother Lincoln (*Duck*) had asthma, Mama was more sympathetic toward him than she was with me. He not only got away with a lot of wrongdoing, he sort of became Mama's ears and eyes on me.

Four

Tommy G., the Bully

ONE DAY WHILE I was coming home from Stuart Middle School, Duck discovered that I was scared of Tommy G, the neighborhood bully. Tommy was bigger and rougher than all the other kids our age. The bad news for me was that Tommy lived directly across the street from our house. While Duck and I were walking home from school that day, Tommy came up from behind us and mugged me to the ground with the intention of putting sand in my hair. Because I was afraid of him, I didn't put up much of a fight as all of the other kids laughed at me as they walked by. Guess who watched the whole thing and couldn't wait to tell Mama? Duck. Somehow, I convinced him not to tell Mama about this episode.

In 1975, the afro was in style and it was very popular to have a clean, long and tight "fro". My Aunt, Roxanne Glover, used to plait (*braid*) my hair until Ma Jennie told Roxanne's beau, Stutson Gary, that she wasn't going to stand for him to be courting or shacking up with Roxanne. It was either marry Rox or stop coming to our house and stay over in Indiantown, Florida, where he was from. That was a no brainer for Stutson. He made a quick and easy decision to marry Roxanne and she didn't plait my hair anymore. Ghuna's sister, Kim, became Turk, Duck, Bean, and Peas' hair beautician.

Since Duck had the goods on me being scared of Tommy, I was on my best behavior, being extra nice to him. After school a few days later, guess who was waiting for me on East Lake Street's dirt road? Tommy the bully. I noticed that as I got closer to him his fists were clenched tight and his face was frowned up with a fighting look. This wasn't the time to talk and there was no room for error leading to a trip and fall. While approaching Tommy, at the very last second, I made my move. I was as quick as Tony Dorsett (*former Dallas Cowboys player*) and as elusive as Barry Sanders (*former Detroit Lions player*) getting away from the neighborhood bully. I didn't know I could run so fast. While the school kids were watching and laughing at me as I made a clean getaway, guess who was standing there looking? Duck.

Later on, Duck and I had a dispute over household chores and because I wouldn't submit to his demands, he let the goods out of the bag that he had on me. In other words, he told Ma Jennie that I was intimidated by Tommy and that Tommy had put sand in my hair. He told her that I was scared to fight the bully. Immediately, Ma Jennie gave me a stern look with some old school choice words. She basically laid the law down by letting me know that if she ever heard again that Tommy or any other kid hit me and I didn't hit or fight them back, she was going to beat me until the cows came home. We didn't own any cows, but I knew what she meant. That same week, my defining moment presented itself during a confrontation

with the bully. While coming home from school, there
he was standing in the middle of the East Lake Street
dirt road (*paved since*) waiting for me. I am sure he was
thinking about how I had "Shake and Baked" him in our
last confrontation. I was thinking *How in the world am
I going to get past this bully now, while all the school
kids and Duck were watching*? As I assessed my situation quickly, my options didn't look good. I was only one
block away from my house, just past Mr. Carter's and Mr.
Gipson's houses. The problem was, Tommy the bully had
positioned himself strategically between me, my house
and a junky field with a very large, deep, and dirty pond
that's also located on East Lake Street and Tarpon Ave.
So, my first option was to run through the field taking a
chance of getting beat up and possibly getting drowned by
the bully.

My second option was even more terrifying, which was
to man up and fight the bully straight up. My third option
was the unthinkable because even if I did manage to get
past the bully, I would still have to face Ma Jennie with
one of her equalizers when I got home for running from
the bully. Within seconds I decided bravely to man up
and fight the bully. Now my unproven fighting skills were
on the spot. Since the objective in fighting is winning,
I was required to do whatever it took — by all means necessary — to be victorious. This train of thought prompted
me to resort to a wrestling tactic I saw Terry Funk, Jr. use
against Dusty Rhodes at a professional wrestling match in
the West Palm Beach Auditorium. Mr. Allen used to take
the guys in the neighborhood who worked with him to the
wrestling matches every Monday night. I was pleasantly
surprised when I realized that watching wrestling greats
like Andre the Giant, the Great Malinko, Pac Songe, Junk

Yard Dog, and Jack and Jerry Briso, the Four Horsemen, Rick Flare, Harley Race, Dorie and Terry Funk, and Dusty Rhodes gave me a valuable resource of fighting strategies to draw from.

With sand cuffed secretly in my right hand, I confronted Tommy the Bully with a renewed confidence knowing that I was going to win this fight convincingly. The school kids and Duck looked on as Tommy the bully made an aggressive move toward me. To Duck's surprise, Tommy's eyes were blinded with a face full of sand and it was on from there baby! After I took him down like the wrestlers I saw in West Palm, I hit him with a quick eight piece (*eight punches in rapid succession*) before he cleared his eyes and came back to his senses. As the bully was going down like the Titanic, I was in the wind on my way home. The school kids and Duck had witnessed my first fighting victory. My record was 1 – 1.

Beating up the bully earned me street cred and a reputation with the neighborhood kids. Finally, standing up to a fight also gained me some school friends in Rudolph Jamison (*Rudy J. or Rudy*), L.D. Atkins, Craig Holmes, and Bernard McCreary. At that point, I decided to nickname the bully and started calling him "Funky G". This name infuriated him to the point where it led to a series of down and dirty fights between us. Eventually, we both developed a mutual respect for each other despite all those crazy, senseless fights.

Five

In the Mix with Rudy J. and Mary J.

IN 1974, I had heard so much about how the impeached President, Richard Nixon had it going on; how he spread the wealth so decently that he earned the name "Tricky Dick". This famed history inspired me to get my second job at The Stuart News on East Ocean Boulevard. I simply applied, then was interviewed and earned myself the paper route I desired in East Stuart. This job trained and taught me about accountability, stewardship and entrepreneurship when dealing with people and money. I sharpened my skills in these areas, along with my salesmanship and I gradually became very manipulative and deceptive with The Stuart News' money.

In my mind, the 75/25 hiring contract agreement[1] wasn't adding up right anymore. I reasoned that I was the one running from the neighborhood dogs, sweating in the hot sun, dealing with the cold weather and sometimes the rain as I distributed the newspapers. In the grand scheme of things I thought, *That ain't right*, as James Brown (*the Godfather of Soul*) used to sing. I thought I had it all figured out and down pat until Ma Jennie got a phone call from The Stuart News' front office. After Mama got off the phone and confronted me about the situation, my first response was to totally deny any wrongdoing. Then when she told we were going to The Stuart News office the next morning, all of a sudden I felt my breath leave my body. Everything around me in the room started to cave in on me. I knew that I couldn't hide or run from Mama. I had to face the music and be held accountable for my actions. I went to bed worried and woke up tired from lack of sleep as the night passed quickly. Before we left home that morning, Mama had a few encouraging words for me. She looked me in my face and said, "Turk, you put yourself in this situation and the only way you are going to get out of it is, you have to be honest and just tell the truth and everything is going to be all right, you hear?" Of course, I said, "Yes Ma'am." It was much easier for her to say those words to me than it was for me to hear them because she wasn't the one who had to assume responsibility. In fact, Ma Jennie reinforced one of her famous sayings around the house which was, "If you make your bed hard, you are the one who has to sleep in it." She always had a way with her ancient words that had significant meanings behind them.

When we arrived in the parking lot at The Stuart News, I wasn't a bit nervous because I was with my hero, Ma Jennie. I didn't know what these people were going to say or do concerning their missing money for which I was responsible, but I had a strong sense of confidence knowing that Ma Jennie wasn't going to let anything happen to her baby boy.

Once we were inside the office, things went a lot smoother than I anticipated. Since their objective was to retrieve their gangster (*"money"*) and I was willing to agree to the specific terms for paying back their money, they were satisfied with the outcome. Mama was proud of me for how I conducted myself in that situation.

In front of my house one Sunday afternoon, Rudy J. asked me if he could share something with me. My first thought was whatever he wanted to share with me must have something to do with drugs, money, or girls. Boy did I miss it big time. I had no idea that I would never forget his next few words. Rudy J. looked me straight in my eyes without blinking and said, "Turk, if you don't repent of your sins, turn from your wicked ways, and receive Jesus Christ in your heart as your personal Lord and Savior, YOU are going to HELL when you die." My immediate response was, "Man you're tripping, where's that good stuff that you've been smoking?" Then, I told Rudolph, "If you don't get out my face and get up off Tarpon, I am going to knock the Hell out of you." To my surprise, he didn't even move and I thought to myself, "This fool must be crazy standing in front of my house talking about me going to Hell."

He didn't know it, but he earned my respect for sharing the truth about something I didn't know anything about. In reality I tried to intimidate him because the things he shared with me convicted my conscience. This confrontation compelled me to do a self-examination to

consider seriously whether there is a God who really loves
me, who has a purpose for my life and doesn't desire for
me to go to Hell.

While I was thinking about the conversation I just
had with Rudolph, there wasn't anything tangible for
me to embrace that would have influenced my decision
one way or the other. For some reason, out of nowhere,
my thoughts reflected upon several families and their
homes that were on my favorite paper route in East
Stuart and Sherwood Forest. Families like the Harvey's
(*Mr. Cowboy*), Mrs. Willie Mae Johnson, my cousins the
Coopers, the Dickens, the Davis', the Fosters, the Bells, the
Christies, Mr. and Mrs. Felix Williams, the McFaddens,
Mr. Wooten (*my fifth-grade teacher*), the Leggetts, and
the Gipsons. There was something special and unique
about their homes that I couldn't put my finger on.

Suddenly, it came to me what they all had in common.
They were all Christian people who believed in the Lord
Jesus Christ. I used to enter their homes once a week to
collect the weekly fee for the papers and I always noticed
a sweet, warm presence in their homes. The atmosphere
in their homes was always peaceful and loving with kind
words spoken therein. By no stretch of the imagination
is this observation a knock on the home environment in
which I was raised. Are you kidding me? I could feel the
sting from one of Ma Jennie's swift back-handed licks
upside my head for even considering a complaint about
my upbringing.

In light of the fact that she raised her family of three
generations with a below average education, Ma Jennie
did a phenomenal job. She loved everybody uncondition-
ally, even the total strangers who didn't have anything to
eat or anywhere to stay. On several occasions, Mama had

allowed strangers to eat at our table, bathe in our tub. She even let those rascals sleep on the front porch or living room sofa. In my mind at the time, I didn't like it, but it wasn't my house, and I was just a twelve-year-old who was smelling his piss, as Mama would say, so I kept my little thoughts to myself. I thought it was the norm in Mama's house to have a chaotic and dysfunctional atmosphere at times. People from all over Martin County would gravitate to Ma Jennie's house for different reasons. Family, friends, in-laws and even the nosey haters would come around our house on weekends and especially on holidays. Everybody knew that the grills would be fired up, alcohol and drugs would be present, and music would be playing as everyone would be sipping and tipping, stopping and copping, and moving and grooving. That is how we lived and rolled on Tarpon. This also explains how I was able to decipher the different atmospheres in those Christian homes so easily.

Though Ma Jennie and her boys attended Macedonia Church often, we didn't understand the Bible clearly, nor did we know what it meant to be saved and to live a Christian life. We did have a reverence and respect for God and His Word, but we weren't willing to turn from our rebellious ways and surrender unto the Lord. In fact, the only time I remember the Bible being open in our home was when Pastor Henry Lewis and his wife, a few deacons, and a few mothers of the church would stop by to encourage us and pray with us. These visits from the church would always touch Mama in a special way because she would often cry during and after prayer. Each time, after the church members left and she calmed down, she would tell me to get a cold one (*lite beer*) for her out of the refrigerator. Since I had to get it, I would usually pop the top and get me a swig or two. Mama and I were cool like that since I was her baby boy. She would often chill out after drinking a cold one and then for relaxation, she would ask me to massage her shoulders and neck. It was always my pleasure to give her a massage because Ma Jennie was my hero.

On other occasions when Mama got really blitzed on her favorite drink, moonshine, she would really lay down some serious trash talk and pop off or share some old fond memories depending on the moment. This happened whenever her friend, Mrs. Mary Gary from Indiantown, would stop by with her chauffeur.

She would often bring a bottle or two of shine from Georgia for them to sip on as they reminisced about their past. These two senior pioneer ladies in their sixties used to carry on like two young girls in their own world. They talked about old friends, places, and things in Georgia and, of course, their deceased husbands, Mr. Turner Gary and Mr. Henry Griffin.

In 1977, at the age of thirteen, I landed my third job at Ding Hou Restaurant—the very first Chinese restaurant in Martin County. I worked full-time in the summer and on weekends, but part time during the school year and when I didn't have baseball practice or a game. I earned a nice check with decent tips from washing dishes and busing tables. This enabled me to buy me and my friends more than one Lilly Dilly (*frozen Kool Aid in a cup*) from Mrs. Maxine, who sold the best Lilly Dillies in East Stuart.

Because I had extra money in my pocket during this season of my life, I started buying marijuana (*Mary J*) and smoking out (*getting high*). Whenever I smoked Mary J, it seemed like another eye opened up in my mind to show me how much more beautiful the world around me was. Under the influence of Mary J, nobody could tell me I wasn't smarter and wiser than my friends and the kids my age. Under the influence of Mary J, I played baseball on a higher skillset level than the kids my age.

The parents of the kids I played against couldn't stand me. They called me "hot dog" and "show off" because I embarrassed and dominated their sons on the field of play when I pitched and/or batted right- or left-handed.

The parents of the kids who played with me didn't have a problem with my hot dogging because their kids looked good winning. They didn't know that I used to be as high as Cooter Brown on Cloud 9 (*under the influence*) and hungrier than a bear because Mary J gave me munchies like crazy. Come on now, if you have ever been under the influence of Mary J, you know exactly what I am saying because you have been there, seen that, and smoked that. If you have never smoked marijuana, good for you; don't you ever try it.

My oldest aunt, Mary Ann Glover (*my mother's sister*), was a weed junkie. I mean home girl had to have her stuff or it was like she was going to have a fit. I really thought that Mary J was Mary Ann's medication because, as far as I could remember from a very young age, she smoked her daily portion like clockwork. Mary Ann always had a slick way with words that made people laugh. Her demeanor was like that of Esther, a character on the 1970s show *Sanford and Son*. You could tell when Mary Ann was good and high because she would often say "watch it sucker" or "child please" as she stared you down with her big pop eyes.

She was quick and sharp with her words of sarcasm. Mary Ann was a chip off the old block of her mother Viola (*my grandmother*) and her grandmother Ma

Jennie's tree, so she could pop off some mean cuss words. Whenever Mary Ann had something that someone else wanted from her and she wasn't in the spirit of giving, her favorite response was "If I do, Moses [from the Bible] will come around the corner riding on a bike." In other words, she wasn't giving up anything and then she would get them out of her face.

Since I was supplying my own weed, I smoked out by myself, but I was becoming paranoid whenever I did so. I decided that I needed a smoking buddy, so I persuaded someone my age who lived in the same hood to get on Mary J with me. My classmate, future best friend and new found smoking bosom buddy was none other than Rudy J—the same joker who told me I was going to Hell. I was no longer paranoid when smoking Mary J because Rudy J was smoking it with me whenever I fired it up.

Each time Rudy and I smoked out I thought that Mrs. Hun (*Rudy's mother*) was going to kill him because she was one of the senior mothers in the church. Rudolph knew his mother didn't want him hanging out with Ma Jennie's boys, but the influence of Mary J was too strong for him to resist.

ENDNOTES

I The contract stated that 75% of proceeds from newspaper sales on my delivery route would go to The Stuart News and 25% of those proceeds would go to me.

Six

Identity Crisis in a Dysfunctional Family

IN THIS SEASON of my life—at the age of thirteen—I found myself searching to identify with something or somebody and the tragedy was that I didn't even know for what or whom I had been searching. My father, "Cool Breeze," was MIA and never told me that he loved me. He only went in half and half with my mother to produce me and financially support my brother and me when we visited him in Belle Glade. So, homeboy wasn't much of a role model for me to look up to or follow. My second oldest brother, Duck, was challenged with the same identity crisis as I was, so he was disqualified from being my role model. Though we loved each other, we definitely had our battles as siblings. Because Duck has asthma, he couldn't get high on Mary J with me. My oldest brother Arthur Glover (*Peas*) wasn't much of a role model either because he was also a weed head and a notorious trash talker. He would cuss you out, talk about your Mama and be ready to fight

29

anybody except Ma Jennie and Ski-Bo (*Uncle Jimmy*).
Everybody in the hood called Peas "Wine Head" because
he was born with blood shot eyes. Also, he was bow-legged
and blacker than tar. I mean my brother, Wine Head,
is midnight black. Only his closest friends and smoke
buddies called him "Daddy Wine." Daddy Wine had a
serious clique of East Stuart characters that he did his
thang with like Daddy Fat (*Gator*), Mr. Cag, Rufus, Coon
Man, Bubba, Grady Shady, Neck Bone, and Soul Bookie.
Wine Head's friends didn't appeal enough to me for me to
embrace or identify with them. Then, there was my fourth
oldest uncle, Arelouis Dale Glover (*Ricky*) who was living
a homosexual lifestyle. I respected Ricky but homeboy was
out there, and I knew without any doubt that I didn't want
any part of that lifestyle. Ricky lived in a smaller house
behind our house. It had a toilet but no shower or bathtub.

One afternoon he decided not to clean out the bathtub
after using it. When Ma Jennie noticed it and discovered
that he was the guilty party, she politely told him to clean
the bathtub. Instead, Ricky got sassy with my hero. Mama
tried to reason with him gracefully and calmly, but he
stiffened his neck in noncompliance and straight up told
Mama what he wasn't going to do. Until this point in my
life, I had never seen anyone mouth off or disrespect Ma
Jennie without swift consequences. I thought to myself
that Mama wasn't going to let this joker off the hook easily
because he had just broken two cardinal rules against the
backbone of our family.

All eyes in the house were watching Mama to see
how she was going to chastise Ricky for his disrespectful actions. We knew that she had several options for
disciplining him, but she pulled out the most physical
equalizer that we had never seen in action. Like the

commander-in-chief at the White House, Ma Jennie picked up the phone to make one call and five minutes later Ski-Bo, the Vietnam Vet, drove up and got out of his car. The look on his face was like that of a man on a mission. When he came into the house, Ma Jennie gave him the low down of what happened and, basically, she authorized him to give Ricky the business — that is, to discipline him. Ski-Bo hit Ricky with a two piece, a body shot and a head shot. When the dust settled for Ricky, he was sporting a broken jaw and a swollen eye.

My youngest uncle, Ralph Glover (*Bean*) was living a rebellious and renegade life. Bean was very sneaky and crafty in his deeds, which always landed him in some kind of trouble. On one occasion while Bean was under the influence of alcohol and Mary J, he crossed the line with Ma Jennie by talking back to her with disrespectful words. Mama gave Bean that look with her hands on her hips. She then picked up the phone to make one call and we all knew what that meant. Five minutes later, Ski-Bo rolled up to the house and before Bean knew anything, Ski-Bo had done stepped in his chest (*got in his face*). Everything happened so fast from my up-close view. Mama's living room quickly turned into Ma Jennie's gym where Ski-Bo put on a fighting exhibition/clinic. Bean was totally overpowered. He took a brutal beating at the hands of Ma Jennie's enforcer. Ski-Bo hit Bean with an eight piece, and it was lights out for Bean. After what I had just witnessed in Ma Jennie's gym, I decided that Bean was definitely not on my radar as a role model for me to follow.

Then there was my third oldest uncle, Charles Glover (*Mickey*) who was also a Vietnam Vet. Mickey was a junkie and a dope pusher who rolled with a ruthless clique of men who didn't see or spare anyone but each other and their families. Mickey's two main partners in crime were Ray Preston and Woodrow Jackson. These three characters didn't play the radio. That is, they meant business. Because the three of them had a serious reputation throughout Martin County, and especially in East Stuart, I called them "Three the Hard Way." They gave fits to Stuart Police Chief and his department. On a few occasions, after they had broken the law, they jumped the police, which made matters worse. They only respected and surrendered to Ma Jennie and two Black officers, Mr. Robert Ware and Mr. John Holmes.

One of the things that caught my attention and began to appeal to me was how Mickey, Ray, and Woodrow were smooth with the ladies. Ray put his Mack down (*he was a good talker*) on my Aunt Mary Ann and they went half on a baby, and out popped Kelvin Preston (*Curl*). Another thing I learned from "Three the Hard Way" was that the hustling game wasn't based on sympathy, and the weak were open game to be had and played on.

Then there was my oldest uncle, O.B., the flamboyant dresser, throwback player, drug pusher, and talented singer with the gift of gab. When everyone else was sporting afros, O.B. was donning a mean processed hairstyle like Jackie Wilson's — "fried, dyed, and laid to the side." O.B. wore expensive, flashy clothes and stacked shoes. He also drove a "Deuce and a Quarter" with fur interior and an eight track to go (*aka "pimp mobile"*).

O.B. had two smooth friends in Ben and Harry Hippy who drove up-to-date Cadillacs. Harry Hippy was more of a gangster criminal who took the oath and code of the game seriously. After the all-night players' parties O.B. used to have at his house in Rio, Florida, he would tell me to come over and clean up. While cleaning his house over in Rio, I used to listen to the latest music on reel to reel and smoke Mary J. The pleasure was all mine because I would find loose money and drugs throughout the house. After cleaning the house, I would watch bootleg films on reel to reel that were rated for adults only. In 1977, I didn't know what Triple-X meant but I knew what it looked like because I was sure locked in a zone while watching it.

The influences for my rebellious lifestyle developed while I lived at Ma Jennie's house as I observed the behavior of the dysfunctional characters who lived in and or visited her house. Though Ma Jennie raised all of us, her only daughter, Viola Glover, was the mother of all of these Hell raisers. Viola resided in Belle Glade where she and her husband, Charles Glover, Sr., birthed Ma Jennie's crew on the scene. My grandfather, Charles, drowned in the back seat of a car in Belle Glade when I was a baby, so I didn't get to know him.

It came to pass that another smooth-talking muck stepper named George Jones introduced himself to Viola. They hooked up and she birthed two more beautiful girls, Alfreda Jones (*Pepper*) and Helen Jones (*Tiny*) whom she raised in Belle Glade.

In our family circle, we called Viola "Fred" for a reason. That is, Fred stands at 5 feet 8 inches with big pop eyes, and she never leaves home without packing her .38 Special. Fred has a quiet Teflon aura about her that keeps her from being moved by small matters. She is a chip off the block of Ma Jennie's tree, which gained her a place of great respect in our family and with others who know her personally. I hated going to Fred's house whenever we visited our parents on weekends in Belle Glade because she watched my every move with her pop eyes. She made it no secret that she knew I was a bad little mannish rascal. In fact, Fred expressed to me on one occasion that Ma Jennie (*her mom*) let me get away with everything, but she wasn't having it while I was there—not in her house! Fred always expressed tough love toward me with sharp words, and she was certainly not sweet on me like Ma Jennie was.

Then there was Irvin Griffin, Ma Jennie's only off-the-glass (*crazy*) and radical son. Irvin was better known in the hood by his nickname, "Nappy Chin" because he wore a bushy beard. He also carried a very sharp Crocodile Dundee-style knife by his side. Homeboy wasn't wrapped too tight upstairs, and it would not take you too long to figure that out if you met him. He was cool as long as nobody came into his space and he didn't feel disrespected. I was so bad when I was growing up, Nappy Chin often told me straight up but jokingly that he should have killed me when I was a baby.

Also, I can't forget my Great Aunt Sally Mae James who was one of Ma Jennie's two sisters. Sally Mae and her husband Andrew James lived in South Philadelphia off of 18th and Washington. Since I was a baby, Ma Jennie and Sally alternated visiting each other's homes every other year. I always looked forward to traveling to South Philly to play in the snow.

It was in Philadelphia that I learned about Ma Jennie's and Sally Mae's past from Uncle Andrew. You see, Uncle Andrew was a real-life comedian on the crazy side who told anybody just what was on his mind. He never sugar coated his thoughts. Before there was ever a Redd Foxx, Richard Pryor, Robin Harris, or Tyler Perry, there was my crazy Uncle Andrew, who was extremely funny, living in South Philly. Andrew shared with me some golden history on Ma Jennie's and Sally Mae's early adult years. They were all born and raised in South Carolina where he met them. Andrew said, "Boy, Jennie and Sally Mae were the talk of the town because they were the finest two Redbones (*light-skinned women*) in South Carolina. He said that every man in town was on Jennie's and Sally's trail, including himself, because he was determined to catch one of them. As Uncle Andrew sipped his favorite brand of whiskey and breathed upon me with his alcoholic breath, he described the beauty of Jennie and Sally in graphic detail. Andrew said that everyone called Jennie "Jennie Slim" because she stood at 6-foot 2-inches tall, had beautiful long silky black hair, attractive eyes, and a gorgeous smile. She was finer than Lena Horne.

Jennie Slim was a trash-talking Redbone who knew she had it going on, and she was a good fighter who knew how to throw her hands. Andrew said Jennie Slim was a sight of beauty to behold, but because she was so elusive, he knew that he'd have to kill her in order to catch her. With a Jack Nicholson joker look on his face, Andrew said, "I am a lover, not a fighter."

He also told me how Jennie Slim would entice men by pulling up her dress to show them her butt and then tell them to come get some. Instead of getting what they wanted, they got a surprise beat down at the hands of Jennie Slim.

Based upon how he witnessed Jennie Slim beat up other men, Andrew said he didn't want to bust a cap in her with his .357 Magnum, so he declined to make a move on Jennie Slim and took his chances with Sally instead.

Andrew said everyone called Sally "Pretty Sally" because she stood exactly 6 feet, had beautiful black curly hair, pretty brown eyes, an attractive face, and a knock out body that made her sexier than Jennie Slim. She dressed jazzier and more elegantly than other ladies in town. Andrew said, more importantly for him, Pretty Sally wasn't a fighter like Jennie Slim which made him more determined that he had to have her.

As Andrew took a swig from his whiskey bottle, he said he always thought that Jennie Slim wasn't wrapped too tight upstairs. Andrew said what really sold him on Pretty Sally was the fact that she wasn't running around pulling up her dress like her crazy sister. With a gleam in his eyes and a smile on his face, Andrew said Pretty Sally was so beautiful that she caused his heart to skip a beat and cut a step like the Temptations. He said that Sally's beauty almost intimidated him, which caused him to act goofy over her, but he couldn't afford to let her see him sweat. Uncle Andrew understood that he only had one good opportunity to catch the desire of his heart and he couldn't screw it up. Andrew told me that when he made his move, there was resistance at first but, eventually, he accomplished his mission and married Pretty Sally.

Meanwhile, at a very young age while growing up, Ma Jennie took me with her to visit my uncles in Florida prisons. We visited O.B. at Avon Park where he did time for robbery and kidnapping. We also visited Mickey at Florida State Prison (FSP) in North Florida, where he did time for selling drugs and battery on law enforcement with Three the Hard Way.

Inside the prisons there was a unique atmosphere and flow of existence that was the total opposite of life in society. Visiting the prisons didn't strike me as a bad place to be. Though it wasn't my dream or desire to do time, this experience numbed the fear factor of ever coming to prison.

Seven

Infatuated with a Bad Master Plan

IT WAS 1978, at the age of fourteen, life was beautiful and fun for me. Having nothing to do one early spring day, I grabbed my BB gun to go hunting. I didn't feel like walking or riding my bike to the nearby woods behind the East 10th Street Recreation Center to shoot birds, so I began shooting at street lights, eventually knocking one of them out. The next thing I knew, I was in the back seat of an officer's police car. As the officers were completing their paperwork on me at the police station Ma Jennie came through the door like the Feds telling them that they weren't taking her boy anywhere. As the officers were trying to explain to Mama their procedures that needed to be followed, she wasn't hearing anything they had to say. Mama was still wearing her cooking apron, sporting her head scarf, and carried a wad of snuff in her bottom lip.

While they were talking, Ma Jennie made her way into the room where I was and hit me with a quick two piece upside my head. She then snatched me up by the collar and we headed for the door as the officers made an attempt to stop her from taking me out of the station. The last words I heard from the officer in charge were, "Mrs. Griffin, your son still has to go to court." As we walked out, Mama told them, "For now, he's going home with me to be chastised."

Since Mama was getting older and I was getting bigger as a teenager, I really didn't mind her beatings because they were much shorter and less abusive. More importantly, she only had to call Ski-Bo on me one time. In fact, it was on this occasion that she called Ski-Bo — after she beat me!

Before he drove up to the house, I thought seriously about running away but the very thought of the brutal beat downs that Ricky and Bean experienced at the hands of Ski-Bo (*Ma Jennie's enforcer*) made me reconsider.

Thank God I followed my right mind because Ski-Bo only counseled me with a serious warning about consequences the next time Ma Jennie should call him to discipline me. Ski-Bo also forbade me from playing in a highly anticipated baseball game between Stuart and Indiantown. That really hurt me and our baseball team because everyone knew I was the best player and without me it was likely that Indiantown would win, which they did.

During my court day for shooting the streetlight out, Mama sat quietly in the audience until the judge started talking about sending me to a detention center. The next thing I knew, I felt Ma Jennie come up from behind me, grab me by the collar and attempt to leave with me, but the bailiff stopped us. When the judge explained his position, Ma Jennie expressed hers. The conclusion was that the judge warned me specifically that the next time I came before him, he was going to send me to the detention center. Ma Jennie was not only my hero; she had become my "lawyer" that day because she got me off the hook.

When football season came around in the Pop Warner League, I played for the Stuart Hornets. Rudolph (*my best friend*) also played for the Stuart Hornets. During this football season, Rudolph and I became interested in girls. Boys and girls played a game on paper in which they would indicate, by checking a box next to "Yes" or "No," whether or not they liked a particular person of the opposite sex. He and I decided that we weren't going to be checking "Yes" or "No" in boxes on paper anymore. That is, Rudy and I decided we were graduating from that level (*infatuation game*) and moving on to the real action (*sex*).

After our first Jamboree game an attractive girl's butt and face caught my attention and it was on for me baby! I fell in love with my first girlfriend from Indiantown. Her name was Rita Graham and she was a brick house just like Lionel Richie sang about. She was finer than all outdoors. The girl had me feeling butterflies in my stomach which I had never experienced before. The relationship was a total infatuation of passionate kisses and hand holding because I never busted the ultimate move on her if you know what I mean.

From this experience, I quickly acknowledged that it costs to be the boss when dealing with females. In other words, it takes flow (*money*) to make certain things happen because females like nice things and desire to be treated like Queens in every respect. It was at this season in my life that I decided to take my game to another level to earn more money in order to do my thang.

I started working with Bean and Wine Head cutting grass for Mr. Charlie Bess. Because we only worked on the weekends and after school, that money was slow and limited me in what I wanted to do.

Visiting my parents one weekend in 1978, I discovered a master plan on how to come up with fast money. It was in Belle Glade ("*the Muck*") where I first heard the song, "For the Love of Money" by the O'Jays, which inspired me along this path.

On a nice day with the smell of Bobby Reds bar-b-que ribs and the unique smell of the Muck up in the air, the music of the O'Jays was pumping out of the Lil Harlem Bar. At the same time across the street a block away, the music of Teddy Pendergrass was booming out of the Cotton Club Bar as the men and women on Fifth Street were selling drugs, and doing their thang (*prostitution*). Personally, witnessing this type of action where the love of money is something serious compelled me to glean a similar shrewd mentality to hustle in that line of business.

Being exposed to this unique atmosphere on the Muck where things moved a lot faster than they did in East Stuart, I was able to connect with the right people to cop Mary J on a larger scale and at a lower price. This meant greater profit and more money to do what I really wanted to do. Though I came up with a money-making plan with a jumping product, the real challenge remained that I didn't yet have any customers. Getting under the influence of my own supply, which was not wise, I drifted into my own think tank to consider my limited options to make the most informed decision to move my product.

Arriving back in East Stuart I realized at the conclusion of my thoughts, that I already had a source of potential paying clients. All this time they were there in front of me—walking to and from school, getting on and off the school bus, getting in and out of cars and going to and from classes. Stuart Middle School was the place where it was going to go down. You heard it right, in my adolescent mind Mary J would enhance my generation's higher educational learning and I would profit from my service. Everyone involved would benefit.

It was the perfect set up and Rudolph thought that I was crazy, but my master plan sure didn't stop him from smoking with me. Rudy was not only my best friend, but he was also my best non-paying customer. Even though he was broke as Joe Turkey, we were "boyz". We were cool like that and down like two flat tires. The only problem was Mary J didn't allow me to factor into the equation the potential consequences if/when a deal goes down wrong. I never told Rudy, but for his own good and because he was my boy, I never put his freedom or life in harm's way as I did my own freedom and life.

Just when business seemed to be booming and things were going smoothly, my teacher informed me that I had to report to the principal's office immediately. As I walked to the principal's office, I made sure that I was clean and straight. All sorts of thoughts raced through my mind as to what could be wrong, but I assured myself that whatever it was I had to be cool and not let them see me sweat.

I will never forget the scene that awaited me upon entering the principal's office. The first faces I noticed were those of the three White jokers (*students I used to call "Larry, Curly, and Moe" from the Three Stooges*) to whom I had sold three sacks (*bags of Mary J*) earlier that day. All three were still as high as Cooter Brown with glossy eyes on cloud nine. Their faces were totally red as all three shook like Rodney Dangerfield.

The next two faces I quickly acknowledged were two sheriff's officers who were wearing looks that indicated I was in some serious trouble. Then, I saw the legendary basketball coach, and highly respected Principal Don Wallen, who was sitting behind his desk with a look of disbelief on his face. On his desk right in front of him were two of the three sacks I had just sold these three clowns. The judge, the cops, and the witnesses were all in the principal's office. It didn't look good for me as I maintained my composure. Mr. Wallen expressed his disappointment with me because on several occasions he spoke with me as a father would with his own son. Mr. Wallen told me things like greatness was down inside of me and that I had a unique talent to do something special with my life. More importantly, I think Mr. Wallen was disappointed with me because I was playing baseball with his oldest son, Mike.

Mr. Wallen finally asked me "What's your story, because these three students have put the finger on you." My first response was to plead the fifth. But after Mr. Wallen counseled me briefly with his "words of wisdom",

I fessed up and assumed responsibility for my actions. My hero and lawyer, Ma Jennie couldn't get me out of this jam. In fact, by the time Mr. Wallen called to inform her about what had happened, I was cuffed, booked and assigned to my first incarceration at the Detention Center in Ft. Pierce, Florida.

The only places I could go outside of my one-man cell were to the shower, the kitchen to eat, the visitation area, and church. To my surprise, at the church service I heard some familiar words. People I didn't know spoke with me about the Bible and prayed with me. Ma Jennie was my only visitor while I was there in Ft. Pierce.

After serving twenty-one days, Ma Jennie was informed to come pick me up. Back in the hood and at school I was labeled a troubled kid who was a bad influence. Other kids were warned, by their parents, to not associate or have anything to do with Mrs. Ma Jennie's boy (*non-family members referred to her as Mrs. Ma Jennie*). Upon reentering Stuart Middle School in the eighth grade, I had to be counseled again by Mr. Wallen in the principal's office in Ma Jennie's presence. Once they got through with the nice preliminaries between the two of them, Mr. Wallen told Mama that I really wasn't a bad kid at all; I just needed a solid structure and disciplined life. Mr. Wallen told me that I wasn't a bad person; I just made some bad decisions that produced consequences I had to face. He encouraged me to put my mistake behind me and to strive for the best that was before me. Then, he basically established some parameters that I had to follow. I had to govern myself with them to make my process of becoming successful a lot easier.

I went on to graduate from Stuart Middle School and moved onto the ninth grade at Martin County High School at age fifteen.

Eight

The Agreement In My Freshman Year

SINCE MY BROTHER, Lincoln Jolly (*Duck*) had asthma, Ma Jennie and Jennie Mae (*our mother*) decided that it was best for him to move in with her to finish his education in Belle Glade. Duck moved in with our mother in Belle Glade the year prior to my freshman year. That move didn't really sit too well with me, but whenever Ma Jennie spoke, that was the law in our family and her word would be done.

On the weekend before I started my freshman year at Martin County, I convinced my mother to allow me to finish my education in Belle Glade. When Jennie Mae and I consulted Ma Jennie about our decision, she wasn't having it at first because I was her baby boy. She softened up a little and asked if that is what I wanted to do and, of course, I said, "Yes Ma'am." Just like a real lawyer, Ma Jennie established some stipulations in her agreement allowing me to move in with my mother in Belle Glade.

She said I had to finish my freshman year at Martin County High School, attend church with her, get a job, and stay out of trouble. Though it was a challenging contract, Ma Jennie knew that her words would be heeded.

Before my mom left to go back home to Belle Glade, we embraced as we kissed each other on the cheek and she wished me the best.

Immediately, I started on my part of the agreement that Sunday before school. I attended church with Ma Jennie to hear Pastor Lewis preach the gospel of Jesus Christ. The service was very uplifting as the mother of the church, Mrs. Willie Mae Johnson kept jumping up and waving her hands as she shouted, "Praise the Lord, Amen." Then, from time to time she would shout, "HALLELUIAH."

After every service Mrs. Johnson and Mrs. Janie Mae (*another church mother*) would have kind, encouraging words for me. They were always telling me that God had a plan and purpose for my life and they could see something special in me. I didn't know what in the world they were talking about, so I asked Mama after church why Mrs. Johnson and Mrs. Janie always had something to say to me. Mama told me that they were the mothers of the church and that it was their duty to encourage the members of the church.

On Monday morning the smell of Ma Jennie's famous bacon, eggs, sausage, grits, and hot buttered biscuits woke us up. It was the first day of school with Wine Head and

Bean who were seniors. As we got dressed for school and ate breakfast, they gave me the rundown on what to expect on the bus and at school. To my surprise at the bus stop on East 10th Street and Tarpon, almost every male was firing up Mary J before Mrs. Lucille Hall drove up in her bus. Daddy Wine was rolling (*hanging out*) with Gator, Mr. Cag and Bean were hanging with Coon Man, Mac Jr., and their clique.

Not knowing what to expect on the first day of school, Rudolph, our friends, and I stayed neutral (*observed our peers from a distance*) before we got into the groove of things that teenagers do in high school. When Mrs. Lucille pulled up in the bus everyone got on and before she drove off, she stood up to give her protocol speech about her bus rules. What would turn out to be a year-long hilarious episode kicked off that first day. Whenever she gave a speech, somebody always had a smart reply—usually it would be Wine Head. The very first day, Mrs. Lucille told Wine Head, specifically, that she wasn't going to put up with his mess during the school year and that she was prepared to tell Mrs. Ma Jennie on him. Before the blink of an eye and just like Clint Eastwood, Daddy Wine fired back with some profane and perverse words. He then said bodaciously, "Now run and tell that," and the whole bus of students erupted with laughter. This was a common scene between Mrs. Lucille and Daddy Wine which, on a couple of occasions, led to temporary suspension from riding the school bus.

Once we arrived at school, I got familiar with all of my classmates and met new friends. I learned quickly that the restrooms and the grassy area in front of the gym were like Woodstock during lunch hours and class breaks. I mean you name it, Mary J, Cocaine, Alcohol, and even sex. Everyone wasn't involved, only the dysfunctional crowd who felt they had nothing to lose. A certain crowd of Black and White students were rolling like that in 1978 and 1979 at Martin County High School.

During the first week of school, I kept good on my agreement with Ma Jennie and got a job at Lord Chumley's at the foot of Roosevelt Bridge.

My freshman year was a unique one to remember for a number of reasons. One that comes to mind is how Rudolph and I noticed how attractive and fine the females had grown over the summer. I didn't know if this assumption came from being under the influence of Mary J, from working out with weights, or from the fact that our testosterone had started to really kick in.

Two of the prettiest and smartest classmates that we acted silly over were Lizzie Mae Newton and Jackie Thurlow. Liz was Black, Jackie was White, and they both were beautiful. They were the hot topic of the guys' conversations because they were the most attractive and popular female students. Because we never made a move on them, they never knew we existed. Come on fellas, we know that infatuated mindset.

For a certain school event I pumped Rudolph up to make a move on this attractive and fine female from Indiantown. Homegirl was stacked real decent in all the right places and my boy Rudy handled his business with her to become the man of the hour.

My most memorable moment happened during our mid-term exam with Rudolph, LD Atkins, Simmie Brown and I left school to get high and rise LD's go cart in East Stuart. It was a fifteen-minute walk both ways and we only had an hour and a half to work with. After about forty minutes, Rudolph began telling us, "Let's go because we have football practice." Rudolph was the starting quarterback, LD was the starting running back, Simmie was a starting corner back, and I was one of the starting linebackers on the freshman football team. When Rudolph saw that we weren't paying him any attention, he took off and left us. When we finally arrived back at school, late for practice, the football team with the coaches were waiting for us. During the practice, the head coach made LD, Simmie, and me pay for it with extra drills and wind sprints.

After practice, the defensive coach decided he wasn't satisfied so he ordered me, LD, and Simmie to run suicide sprints. The more I ran, the more I kept hearing the Godfather of Soul, James Brown, in my mind saying, "This ain't right." While the coaches and the team were on the sidelines watching, halfway through the drill, as LD and Simmie began to pull away from me, my body agreed with the thoughts in my mind and I began to shut it down. Then, the coaches began yelling at me, "Don't stop, Jolly, keep going. Don't let the team down."

At that moment everything and everybody went into slow motion. Standing bent over with my hands on my kneepads gasping for air on the heated field, I looked at the sideline and all my teammates' mouths and hands were motioning to me to keep going and to not give up. The last three faces and mouths I saw were those of Rudolph, LD, and Simmie saying in slow motion together, "Turk, don't do it! Come on man! Don't quit!" while the sweat was popping off my face with a crazy look in my eyes.

Us being "boyz," they knew that my mind was made up. Standing upright and still breathing hard from the suicide sprints without regaining my composure, a glimpse of the Muck and the hood of East Stuart leaped up out of me. Violently, I slammed my helmet and shoulder pads to the ground as I popped off some profane bombs before heading to the locker room.

After I took a shower and cooled off, I apologized to Rudolph and the team for letting them down. Though they accepted my apology, and we were boyz, they still thought that I was crazy. Despite a drama-filled freshman year, I still managed to stay out of trouble to complete ninth grade successfully and move on to tenth grade.

Nine

Leaving the Party on 9/11 for the Muck

MY MIND WAS on moving to Belle Glade my whole freshman year and throughout the summer. However, it looked like Ma Jennie had reneged on our agreement because my sophomore year was to start in one week.

It was September 11, 1979, three days before school started. That day was special for two reasons, first, September 11th is my birthday and I would turn fifteen that year, and second, surprisingly, Duck showed up at the party to tell me that Mama had come to take me back to Belle Glade. Immediately, I left the party and went home excited to pack all my belongings.

Ma Jennie was happy for me but at the same time her heart was sad that her baby boy was leaving. Jennie Mae was thrilled to see Ma Jennie honoring her agreement, but she was also concerned about how she was really taking it to see the last child she raised leave. Before I left East Stuart, I went back to the party to tell my best friend

Rudolph that I was leaving. He thought that I was playing, but when he walked back to my house with me and saw my mother and all of my stuff packed, he knew that I was serious.

Upon arriving on the Muck in Belle Glade, Mama laid down the law with the house rules and curfew hours. After talking with her, I visited my father. Since my parents were separated, getting acquainted with them in different homes was all new to me. My father, Wenzel Jolly, was better known in the hood as Cool Breeze.

Though Cool Breeze wasn't active in my early life, we still established a good relationship with each other. My dad was a fan of boxing greats Joe Frazier, Ken Norton, and Muhammad Ali. He was a construction worker and a cane field worker who kept ten sharp machetes at his front door and ten at his back door. He said they were presents for anyone who decided to break into his house.

I waited a few weeks before visiting Fred's house because I knew she was waiting to give me a piece of her mind and I didn't feel like hearing it or seeing her pop eyes staring me down. Jennie Mae worked at the U-Save grocery store. She cooked really well, but I missed Ma Jennie and her famous breakfasts and dinners.

Upon entering Glades Central High School, I noticed that the administration and student body were predominantly

Black, unlike Martin County, which was predominantly White. The atmosphere was not only unique, but the mindset and swagger was on a totally different level than that of East Stuart. I had to pinch myself for a reality check because I had never seen so many beautiful sisters my age in one place—especially at school. Duck and our two youngest aunts, Pepper and Tiny, were also attending Glades Central. They told me not to get too loose and to behave myself because they knew that I was going to make something happen.

The first day of school, I got familiar with my classes and made a few new friends. After school I was off to Glades Central's football practice. Our team was called the Raiders. Head Coach Willie McCoy gave us the team speech about his expectations of winning the state championship, which if not won would mean the season would have been an unacceptable failure in the eyes of the community of Belle Glade.

After Coach McCoy addressed the team, he instructed us to report to the field house to get our football gear. I sprinted with everyone else to the building because it was "first come, first served," to get the best stuff. Upon getting all my gear I was challenged with giving it up because I was the only unknown team member who came out to make the varsity team.

It was my moment to make a statement and to establish the fact that I was a bona fide Muck-stepping Hell raiser just like every one of them. With that thought in mind, I got off throwing hands first against another team member. We thumped and rocked and rolled for a few minutes before Randy Phillips, Louis Oliver, and a few others broke us up. Then, one of the guys said, "Where are you from, fool?" Proudly, I let them know that I was born at Glades General, my mom, Jennie Mae, lived on B Place, My grandmother, Viola, lived on 8th Street and my dad, Cool Breeze, lived on 9th Street. It turned out to be my homecoming initiation because everybody started giving me high-fives and chest bumps. Harold Posey was the teammate I fought. His dad and my dad rolled together in the 60s and 70s. In fact, our fathers were neighbors on 9th Street. Ironically, Harold and I became close friends through a fight.

The next thing the football team wanted to know was where I had attended school for the first nine years. When I told them "Martin County," the team nicknamed me "Martin County." From then on, in school and in the hood, I was to be known as "Martin County."

Growing up without a solid structured life and no true identity I began to compare East Stuart with Belle Glade in an effort to find my place and get in where I fit in. I had several options to choose from for getting involved with certain things for entertainment. However, I chose to remain neutral.

Early in my sophomore year I decided to put my best foot forward to make my parents proud of me by staying focused on school and playing football. The pep rallies in the school gym were the highlight of each week. Everyone looked forward to those rallies before each Friday night football game. The Muck Bowl between Belle Glade and Pahokee is a bittersweet, intense rivalry which is a mandatory event for bragging rights. Many spectators come from near and far to witness the Muck Bowl. They come to enjoy a great football game and eat great food. To play football for the Raiders is an honor for every young man because it not only gives them a sense of pride and respect, but also notoriety and popularity. More importantly, it also presents them with a golden opportunity to play for major universities with the possibility of moving on to the NFL.

I played with a few guys who made it to the next levels, like Randy Rutledge (*Baylor*), Ray McDonald (*Gators-UF*), Louis Oliver (*Gators, Dolphins*) and Jessie Hester (*Seminoles, Raiders*). Being on the football team with the nickname Martin County proved to have its benefits. Word got out that Martin County wasn't claimed in school or chosen in the hood by a female.

During lunch at school one day, a beautiful Cuban girl named Sandra Gonzalez made it known that she was about me and that her eyes and heart were fixed on Martin County. I didn't take her too seriously for a few weeks but when she assured me that she was a virgin, it was really on from there between us. Sandra worked at Glades Pharmacy after school and on weekends.

Whenever an opportunity to make some money presented itself to me, I handled my business with pharmaceutical drugs. A few months later in the hood, I cut into (*entered into a relationship with*) a shrewd, attractive lady named Linda Jones who was twelve years my senior. Linda and I definitely had a thing going on as she provided what I needed and wanted financially, materially, and physically. Life was real sweet for me on the Muck. Sandra was my girl in school and Linda was my lady in the hood.

In 1980, at the age of sixteen, I moved on to eleventh grade and found my life drifting in another direction. Because of a serious shoulder injury from playing linebacker, I couldn't excel at my level of play, so I started rolling with people "in the know" circle that "had it like that" in the underground world. Big Don was a close friend of our family who pulled my coat by putting skin on my cap (*imparted knowledge*) to the pros and cons of the drug game upon the air (*5ᵗʰ Street*).

It was Big Don who introduced me to the nightclub life and live concerts in South Florida. I was with Big Don and his posse when I first saw Kool and the Gang, The Whispers, and Maze featuring Frankie Beverly live at the Sunrise Musical Theatre, Ft. Lauderdale, Florida. Sitting on the front row in this type of atmosphere advanced my sixteen-year-old mind and maturity level prematurely. My life seemed to accelerate in the fast lane as I became accustomed to doing things my way—with a rebellious attitude.

During one of Big Don's all-night after parties, he introduced me to NFL greats Ricky Jackson (*Pitt, Saints, 49ers*) and Hugh Green (*Pitt, Bucs, Dolphins*). To my surprise, two of the defensive coaches on the Glades Central staff, McKelton and Summers, were standing right there looking at me.

Coach Summers was my Social Studies teacher and he definitely had a stern warning for me in a private meeting between us at school. It was simple and to the point—"Straighten up and get your act together" or he was "going to personally kick me off the team."

During the third week of football season, I was rolling with Big Don in a popular nightclub in West Palm Beach in the afterhours. I couldn't believe my eyes when I saw that coach Summers and McKelton were also in the club. They believed what they saw because the look in their eyes was as though I had really crossed the line this time.

Upon going to school that week, I was informed by the coaching staff that I was dismissed from the team. With this blow, another chapter in my life began to take place.

One weekend while visiting Ma Jennie in East Stuart, I met an aggressive, fine young female in hot pants named Trina Crosby who lived across the street. We got acquainted real fast and started something between us. After visiting Ma Jennie and spending time with Trina over the weekend, it was time to get back to the Muck for school.

As time went by, back in Belle Glade, I found myself in the middle of some female drama at the White Pool Room on Fifth Street with one of my boys I rolled with, Harold Jackson and his girl Mini. Since Mini couldn't stab Harold Jackson, she stabbed me twice, once on my left forearm and once on the back of my left upper arm before I caught her with a two piece upside her head. Before I could hit her with a more serious combination, she took off like Flo Jo out of the White Pool Room. I didn't realize that I had been cut seriously until Duck started tripping out when

I got home. I was losing so much blood that Duck got scared because our mother wasn't home. Wisely, he called Fred to take me to the hospital. This was the first time I was really glad to see Fred and her pop eyes.

As the doctor stitched me up Fred stood right by my side like she was the surgeon in charge. Though I acted bravely, her presence really gave me a sense of confidence that everything was going to be all right.

I received thirty stitches and was placed on bed rest for a week. My girl Sandra stopped by before and after school daily to check on my recovery. She was more hurt and shook up than I was even though I was the one who had been stabbed and was lying in bed. She was very sweet and supportive while helping me back to health and running errands for me.

On the first day walking back to school after my week-long bed rest, I discovered that word on the street was that my Mom (*Jennie Mae*) was on the hunt for Mini, with a gun, for stabbing her son. Since my mom was well known and liked in the community, the people, in the know, defused the situation.

At this time in my life, I wasn't playing football and wasn't involved in other school activities. Therefore, I found myself getting more involved in pushing drugs and rolling in the nightclub life.

Ma Jennie called one day to tell me that I needed to come back to Stuart ASAP because Trina was saying that she was pregnant by me. This news really rocked my world because I knew that I wasn't ready for fatherhood.

When I arrived back in Stuart, Trina was standing in Ma Jennie's front yard waiting on me, smiling, and crying tears of joy. Though she wasn't showing yet, she sure did put on weight in all the right places.

Going back and forth from Stuart to Belle Glade wasn't cutting it and something had to give. It was 1981, I was in Stuart, the baby was due soon and I had taken my hustling game to another level on Tarpon to make the money we needed. I had brought the shrewd game from the Muck to Stuart to move the wanted product more effectively.

On July 29, Trina rolled up on me and Brinda Jackson as we were flirting with each other in a hallway at the Cherokee Motel. Though the fourth of July had passed, there were fireworks and a cat fight as Trina started popping off profanity at Brinda and me. As I stood between Trina, her sister Lil Moma and Brinda, somehow Brinda managed to push Trina to the ground. Trina's water broke from the impact of the fall, so she had to be rushed to Martin Memorial Hospital. My first daughter, Yashekia Carter, was born prematurely later that same afternoon, July 29. We called her Wenchie because she was so small at birth. I suspected that Trina's mother, Mrs. Velvet, didn't like me. One night I thought I struck a nerve with her and she proved me right by threatening me with a knife and some choice words because I was a little rough on Trina.

Ten

Doing Time
for the Crime

BACK IN BELLE Glade before my senior year I was arrested for selling drugs by "Secret Squirrel" (*the police department's special drug detective*) in front of the Lil Harlem Bar. I tried to run but only a very few have ever outrun the Squirrel and I wasn't one of them. He earned the name Secret Squirrel from the streets because he could outrun 97% of the people he chased. While Secret Squirrel was chasing another drug dealer to arrest, in a last-minute attempt to escape from the police car's backseat while in handcuffs, Lil George opened the back door and everybody on 5th Street screamed "RRRUUUNNN Martin County!" As I stumbled and got out of the car to run a few steps, guess who caught me? Secret Squirrel. The scene was extremely dangerous and chaotic as everybody expressed their concern boldly for my failed attempt to escape.

I was incarcerated at the West Palm Beach detention center until I was committed to the Okeechobee Boys Home. I turned seventeen while in the detention center and was sentenced to service ninety days at the Okeechobee Boys Home.

Upon arriving there, I was orientated as to how to complete their program successfully. After my orientation I was immediately confronted by a gang leader with his rules for initiation. Because I refused to join his gang, it was mandatory that I fight him and one of his gang members.

I figured out my predicament quickly and Ma Jennie's boy got off first and real decent (*landed some good licks*). In the midst of fighting, one of them hit me on the head with a two-by-four. Though the lick caused me to see a few tweety birds, I didn't go down as I stood my ground. Standing up for myself and not being intimidated or bowing down to the gang leaders, I earned myself much respect and dormitory cred where I lived. All the dormitories were named after Presidents of the United States. I lived in the Kennedy dorm.

While at Okeechobee Boy's Home, I enrolled in school to stay focused on getting my education and attended Sunday morning church services. During my stay at the boy's home Ma Jennie visited me twice a month. It was always refreshing for me and a joy to my heart to see her beautiful face as I held her hands and talked with her.

After earning the total 14,000 points I needed to complete the program, I was released just in time for Christmas on December 23, 1981. Wine Head and Ma Jennie came to pick me up and I convinced Wine to drive straight to Belle Glade so that I could take care of some business secretly.

Arriving back in Stuart, I reunited with Trina and the baby. I re-enrolled in Martin County High School to start my senior year in January 1982. Rudolph and our classmates were thrilled to see me again. They tried desperately to recruit me into joining the U.S. Army with them. I wasn't trying to hear that because I acknowledged that we all were traveling on different roads in life.

My brother Duck had entered the Army the previous year. I wished him well, but I had made up my mind that I didn't want anything to do with Uncle Sam and His army. I heard Muhammad Ali tell the media that he "'ain't got no quarrel with them Viet Cong." The war was the United States' problem, not his, so he wasn't fighting their war and I wasn't either.

To come up with some fast money, I tried my luck with gambling on jai alai in Ft. Pierce and dog racing at the Palm Beach Kennel Club. After several weeks of unsuccessful experiences with "Big Jack" (*an illegal gambling numbers pusher*), I washed my hands with the legalized public scam.

In March I was arrested for violating my probation and was locked up in Martin County Jail for two months. The only visits I received were from Ma Jennie and Trina on a weekly basis. While there one day during a dice (*gambling*) game, a notorious fighter named Harliss White (*Grady Shady*) threatened to beat me up if I didn't fight Ghuna for drowning my Uncle David Lee back on July 4, 1970. It was mandatory that I fight Ghuna because

I knew that I couldn't beat Shady. It was crazy but I had to do what I had to do.

After getting out, it didn't take me long to get back into the groove of things on Tarpon. As the game and flow began to boom for me, Trina informed me that she was pregnant again. I was just beginning to learn how to become a father, which included learning how to change Wenchie's diapers. With this news I was compelled to re-evaluate my life because I knew I was in the wrong profession, and sadly I didn't have the inner strength to stop. I seriously considered squaring up to do the right thing because I sensed that something bad was about to happen.

Trina's water broke mysteriously in August, her seventh month of pregnancy. Once again, she had to be rushed to Martin Memorial Hospital. Just like with her first pregnancy, I was there at the hospital with her when our second daughter, Amanda Jolly, was born. Because of complications at birth, we had no other option but to accept the cold announcement that rocked and changed our lives forever. The words that came from the doctor's lips hit Trina and I with the force of a category 5 hurricane—"Amanda won't make it."

Shortly thereafter Amanda passed away peacefully. She had been alive for about twenty minutes. I embraced Trina who was lying in the bed and we both wept tears of grief while in each other's arms. I left the hospital crushed as anger and bitterness gripped my heart and mind.

While Trina and I were arranging the funeral, my Uncle Mickey came from Tallahassee and gave me a grocery bag full of money to pay for all the medical and funeral expenses. Trina and I decided to have a graveside funeral for Amanda at the Fernhill Cemetery.

After the funeral I felt an urgency to just get away from everybody and everything, including Stuart and Belle Glade. The next day, Mickey asked me, "Do you want to make some real serious money, boy?" I was all in on it no matter what the scenario, or consequences, were. I just wanted to get away from everyone and everything. After talking with Mickey, I was assigned to drive, pay close attention to instructions and details, and keep my mouth shut.

When it came time for us to leave for Tallahassee and Panama City, Ma Jennie had a last-minute word of prophecy for us. First, she asked me, "Turk, why are you packing those clothes and where are you going?" As she waited for an answer, Mickey drove up in a rental car with his girlfriend, Bonnie Davis. When Mickey came into the house to get me, Ma Jennie told him not to take me with him. Before Mickey could say anything, I was walking past her with my grip bag (*overnight bag*) on my shoulder as Mickey followed me outside. Then as we stood there looking at her, she pointed her aged, respected finger at Mickey and said, "If y'all get into that car something bad is going to happen." Ma Jennie's words were spoken so profoundly that we knew in our hearts that somehow her words would ring true. Though a strong conviction rested upon my heart and mind, I forced myself to numb Mama's words out and got into the car.

As Mickey drove off, the wisdom of Ma Jennie's words and our worst nightmare began to unfold before our eyes. When we stopped at a rest stop in Orlando, Mickey told me to get behind the wheel and drive. While I drove, we passed Mary J back and forth as Bonnie dozed off to sleep in the front seat. As the car became silent, Mickey dozed off to sleep in the back seat. While approaching Daytona,

Florida at 70 MPH on I-95 North, I also fell asleep at
the wheel. When the car started spinning out of control,
I woke up to Bonnie screaming and Mickey hollering.
Bonnie was screaming Mickey's name repeatedly at the
top of her lungs and Mickey was hollering, "Keep your
hands on the wheel, fool!" The car spun around several
times on the wet road before we stopped in the midst of
heavy traffic.

It was only by the grace of God that no other vehicles
hit us as we faced southward toward northbound vehicles
coming toward us. The vehicles heading toward us simultaneously slowed down to a stop. As I sat there totally
shocked, Mickey got out of the back seat quickly, opened
the driver's side door, snatched me from behind the wheel
and hit me with a three piece as he shoved me into the
back seat.

As Mickey drove on northward, Bonnie cried, begged,
and pleaded with him like a mad woman to turn around
and take us back home. Being the Vietnam veteran Mickey
was, he wasn't hearing it or having it. The objective of
this mission was to come back to South Florida with some
major flow.

Arriving in Tallahassee at his partner Harry Johnson's
townhouse, two grocery bags full of twenties, fifties, and
hundreds were waiting for pick up by Mickey. Harry tried
to convince Mickey to go back home with that flow but
after a brief conversation, it was decided that we were
rolling I-10 westbound to Panama City to handle some
unfinished business.

Once we all (*Mickey, Bonnie and I, and Harry and his
wife Diamond*) arrived in Panama City in separate cars,
we checked into separate hotel rooms on the beach. Six
hours later while Bonnie and Diamond stayed behind in

the rooms, Ma Jennie's words began to come to pass right before our very eyes because Mickey stubbornly refused to abandon the getaway car, we (*Harry and I*) agreed to ditch after the lick (*crime*), and he was the first one of us (*Harry and I*) to get arrested for armed robbery.

Harry and I were trailing Mickey miles away from the crime scene we created and left at Panama City Beach when Mickey was stopped for a routine traffic check. This joker, Mickey, didn't even have a legal driver's license and now he was in Panama City jail.

Meanwhile, Harry and I checked into a Travelodge motel with more money than we could count. Then, Harry got hungry and walked to a McDonald's several blocks down the street to get us something to eat. Thirty minutes later the phone rang in the motel room where I was counting Jacksons, Grants, and Franklins (*dead presidents on twenties, fifties, and hundred-dollar bills*). My first reaction was not to answer the phone because nobody knew I was there but Harry. When I did answer, Harry said "Don't say one word, just listen—I am in jail with Mickey, because I have the key to the motel room, they know where you are, so get out of there right now and try to leave town." The problem for me was that I didn't know where to run to because I had never been to Panama City. Minutes later, from a nearby wooded area, I watched the police swarm the entire area looking for me.

Several hours later, before sunrise, I managed to get to a pay phone to try and call Bonnie and Diamond at the Beach. Because of the stress on my brain from the danger of the situation, for the life of me, I couldn't remember the name of the hotel or its phone number. As I looked around inside the phone booth on Magnolia Street, I noticed several police cars pulling up to where I was. A sense of panic overshadowed me. I felt like a trapped rat because I couldn't get away. Ma Jennie told us that something bad was going to happen. We should've listened but it was too late into the crime now because it was all going down right before my eyes. I could hear Ma Jennie's voice in my mind saying, "I told you not to get into that car." With that thought, the sound of sirens and sight of flashing lights snapped me back to reality.

Looking from inside the phone booth, I saw the police officers get out of their cars with their guns drawn while threatening to shoot if I moved. Carefully directing me out of the booth, they ordered me to lay face down on the road. One of the officers really let me have it by calling me the N-word several times as he put his shotgun barrel to my head. Immediately I felt like passing gas and letting loose some "you know what" all over myself. In my mind I said, "Lord please don't let this fool pull that trigger."

I was roughed up a little as they hauled me off to jail. After being booked, I was interrogated by detectives for wanted information. Using one of their tactics to influence me to sing like Sammy the Bull,[1] they brought in some hot, good coffee and some delicious donuts. Once I got full, I went "Nut City" and pleaded the fifth in a secluded room full of detectives. They really became unglued as one of them grabbed my face and threatened me verbally when he said, "You are going down hard for a long time if you don't cooperate." Mr. Henry and Ma Jennies' beatings prepared me for this abuse, so I was good under their minor pressure. When they were convinced after several hours that I wasn't going to sing like Sammy, they transferred me to the detention center because at the age of seventeen I was still considered a juvenile.

We were charged primarily with three robberies in Panama City and four in Tallahassee. We also became prime suspects in every unsolved robbery from Ocala to Panama City.

During the first week of September 1982, the lead breaking headline news in South Florida was: "Three South Florida men from Martin County, Harry Johnson, Charles Glover, and Adam Jolly, have been arrested on a spree of armed robberies in Panama City and Tallahassee.

Several days later on September 11th, when I turned eighteen, I was adjudicated as an adult and was transported immediately to the Panama City Jail. I received mail from Trina weekly, expressing her love for me and how no man could touch her with a ten-foot pole.

Thirteen months later in October 1983, after traveling back and forth from Panama City to Tallahassee to address cases pending in both jurisdictions, I received four years in Tallahassee to run concurrently with the twenty-five years I received in Panama City. I really didn't feel so bad because Mickey received one life sentence and Harry received three life sentences. The three of us were then transferred to the Lake Butler, Florida Department of Corrections (DOC) for orientation. My DOC number 091132 was assigned to me for life. Every prisoner receives his or her own personal DOC number and from that point forward he or she is identified as a number or inmate rather than a person or human being.

Following orientation, we were brought to the Butler Transit Unit (BTU) before our final destination to serve our time. I was at BTU when I found out that the ten-foot pole Trina spoke about in her letters had been cut down.

During my first collect phone call with Trina from the BTU, her mother took pleasure in telling me "Please don't call my house anymore because Trina has found herself a good man who's not a jailbird." Fellas, you know those words felt like a Mike Tyson body blow. It wasn't a "Dear John" letter, it was Trina's behind-the-scenes hateful mother who dropped the bomb informing me that a man named Jody had gotten my girl and that they had moved on. Getting this kind of news really rocked my world, especially after having just received a twenty-five-year sentence. The lyrics from James Brown's song came to my mind again—"That ain't right."

When the morning came for me to leave for my destination to serve my time, Mickey told me to make sure that I get myself a weapon of destruction (*a knife*) to protect myself and to do so by all means necessary. He also told me to take the crime to any fool (*hurt them before they hurt me*) who tries me in any disrespectful way. Mickey let me know that prison life isn't based upon sympathy for anyone and that only the swift, wise, shrewd, and strong survive in that ruthless environment. His last words were Be strong and be a man as you stand your ground and handle your business." Immediately after Mickey gave me those words, and we embraced, I hit him with a hard right cross to his chest for the twenty-five years I got for following him.

Upon arriving at Sumter Correctional Institution in
Bushnell, Florida, I quickly acknowledged that prison
life is truly another world within this world. Sumter was
classified as the "Gladiator School" and or the "Baby Rock"
because of the constant violence and senseless deaths that
happen there in comparison with Florida State Prison in
Jacksonville, otherwise known as "The Rock."

On my first night after the standard orientation, trouble presented itself in the form of a confrontation in the
living area of the dormitory. It was the prison mentality
code and mandatory initiation ritual for new inmates to
be tested, tried, and proven upon arrival at Sumter. This is
to determine whether you are a man who is willing to die
protecting your pride, dignity, and most importantly, your
manhood. It didn't matter where you were from, each new
inmate was tested to see what he was made of and where
he stood, i.e., to see whether he was a man or a coward.

Each inmate vibed in a certain clique while serving
his time. You were either going to get put down on (confronted) or you were putting down on somebody else,
getting hustled or hustling someone else, paying for protection or someone was paying you for protection. There
was no neutral ground. You either got in where you fit
in, or the business was coming to you. I think you get the
picture.

While I was making up my bed and getting my things
in order, the put down business approached me in the
form of three inmates talking smack. When one of them

came into my space within an arm's distance, I hit him with a serious two piece, letting them know that I was putting up a fight. Very swiftly as they surrounded me, one of them asked, "Where are you from fool?" I told them, "Thats none of your business," as I positioned my back to the wall. Then, one of them pulled out a knife and said, "If you don't tell us where you are from and what city you represent, you are going to be a dead man."

With my back to the wall and a pillow case in my hand while facing three mad thugs who were looking for a knife fight, as well as a hostile crowd that was looking on, my options didn't look too good. So, wisely I complied and told them that I was from the Muck and I wasn't going down like that. Then, one of them said to someone in the nearby crowd, Go and get T-Man." As they held me at knife point, one of them said If T-Man don't know you or your people, we are going to kill you and then we are going to rape you." This was definitely not the time to try any of the wrestling stunts I saw at the West Palm Beach Auditorium. These jokers risked getting their heads peeled back to the fat white meat and losing their lives in this spot over senselessness. As the RPMs of my blood pressure shot up, I was anxious and ready to give my best effort to survive. Then, all of a sudden, I heard a voice in the crowd say, "Back off my homeboy—that's Martin County—he's from the Muck." It was Bill Will from Belle Glade and T-Man from West Palm Beach. They both had Gladiator cred at Sumter and both had come to watch my back and witness my initiation at the Baby Rock.

T-Man asked the three thugs, Which one of you is going to give my homeboy a straight up fade (*fight*)?" When one of them stepped up, it was on as we got it down and thumped for a few minutes. It wasn't a win or lose but everyone knew that Ma Jennie's boy wasn't a coward. He was one who could stand in the paint and represent (*basketball term for giving one's full effort*).

On my first weekend, while at the gym, I had my second fight over some weights with another inmate, Cedric (*"Ced"*) Vernon, who was from the South Side of Jacksonville, Florida, otherwise known as "The Bangum where they Hangum." After our confrontation, during which we both got off what we had on our chests, we became gladiator brothers.

Meanwhile at Sumter, I attended the Chapel Christian Services. I never made a commitment to accept Jesus because Ma Jennie taught her boys to always reverence and respect God and His Word. So, I was taught that if you are not serious about accepting Jesus and serving God faithfully, don't play with the big man upstairs. I believed in giving God some of my time by attending Sunday morning services and that's where I stood.

I received my GED in March 1984. Later that year, I obtained my vocational certificates in basic architectural drafting and in air conditioning and heating (HVAC).

It was late 1984 when twelve hundred dangerous young gladiators watched the movie *Scarface*. That movie literally inflamed every ego, including mine, to be like Tony Montana in some capacity. Scarface was the topic of everybody's conversation for several months to come.

A few days after the 1985 Super Bowl between the Dolphins and the 49ers, word got to me that some trouble was coming from the 305 (*area code*) out of the Dirty South (*Miami*) against Ced (*my partner in crime*). This confrontation was my third knife fight with some fools from Miami who had a beef with Ced and me.

When this potential death fight went down, Ced got banged up and nicked up badly. Thankfully, we both survived our war with those fools. They wanted me to abandon Ced so they could kill him, but I put my life on the line to not let it go down like that. Without even thinking rationally, I responded immediately and violently to keep those fools at bay until my reinforcement showed up. This is how we rolled at Sumter — keeping it real by being our brother's keeper.

In the prison system a man's word consists of all he has, which is his most valuable asset. Anybody can talk a good talk but when the rubber hits the road, actions speak volumes louder than words.

My last fight at Sumter was with a hype man (*someone who starts a fight and runs away as five to seven others come to finish the fight*) from Ft. Lauderdale. He was trying to get some cred off me, but it wasn't happening as I beat the breaks off him. I had to flee out of B-Wing in C-Dorm because his homeboys tried to bum-rush me when they saw that the fight was over.

In a retaliatory move early one Saturday morning around 2:30 a.m., three of them surrounded my bed while I was asleep and one of them put a knife to my throat. Only by the grace of God did they speak just a few crazy words and then took off. This encounter taught me personally to sleep light while doing time in DOC. After that episode, I began attending church services more regularly.

While I was at Sumter for three-and-a-half years, Ma Jennie made sure that somebody chauffeured her to visit her baby boy every six months. Somehow, she sensed or knew that I had been getting into fights. As always, she had words of wisdom for me. Seeing Ma Jennie's beautiful face and holding her warm, smooth hands as we talked inspired my heart with a strong sense of survival, and resolve, to do my time.

In May 1986, Ced and I were involved in our second compound riot at Sumter along with 215 other men. Afterward, we realized that every one of us in confinement had been beat down by one of the members of the riot goon squad. Following that second riot, Sumter Administration transferred all 215 of us to the then newest and most dangerous prison in the state of Florida, Martin Correctional Institution (Martin C.I.) located in Indiantown, Florida. It was home for me because I was only fifteen minutes away from Ma Jennie's house.

When the DOC bus stopped in the sally port[2] at Martin C.I., everyone felt the electricity of the demonic forces in the atmosphere. The look in everyone's eyes indicated that we had arrived at the "big house"—a very serious place. The dark reality was that Martin C.I. was built to be a death trap for any man who failed to adhere to the convict code or who didn't play by the treacherous rules of the game. Martin C.I. was truly another planet on this planet. It was like the Planet of the Apes, Gorillas, and Killers.

Daily, busloads came from the formerly most dangerous prisons such as Florida State Prison (FSP) and Union (*a/k/a, "the Rock"*). I'm talking about 1,400 of the most violent men who were ready to explode like time bombs. These convicts were skillful in hurting and killing people. They had no remorse nor regard for life whatsoever. Life at Martin C.I. didn't discriminate; no one was exempt from the madness, not even the blind, crippled, handicapped, or crazy. The strong thrived on the weak and gullible by intimidating and invoking fear in them.

A different territory of demons lived at Martin C.I. in the hearts of men, which influenced and controlled their criminal mindset and actions. I am talking demons of extortion, lasciviousness, homosexuality, rape, robbery, suicide, and murder that were running rampant and in full force. It was nothing to see a desperate man running from a determined man who was chasing him with a weapon of destruction, be it a very sharp lawn mower blade, knife, ice pick, or even a bat, to kill his intended victim.

I was definitely wired up with an extortion demon to survive under the convict code. Twice I had to yield to a killing demon to protect myself, but I never murdered anyone.

I had no option but to do what I had to do in my space, and it was nothing nice. It was the norm to see a helicopter at least once a week air lifting another seriously injured or potentially dead man out of the Martin C.I. danger zone. This was the norm at Martin C.I. and this was how it went down behind the DOC line. It was only by the grace of God that I survived the madness. Just when I needed a boost of inspiration to strengthen me in the cesspool of this venomous environment, Ma Jennie would visit me with her warm words of love and wisdom. She always encouraged me by saying that everything would be all right and to keep my head up.

In June 1986, I attended a church service in which a familiar prison ministry, Church of God by Faith, came out from East Stuart. After the service the preacher asked the security officer to call Adam Jolly over to him. I was a little embarrassed as I walked toward him in front of about two hundred men who were very curious as to what the preacher wanted with Jolly. It was Mr. Eugene Dickens and he said, "Great day boy, my daughter Anna thought she recognized you." Part of his family and the Bell family came to minister the Word of God in their prison ministry. The Bell family is known as a devout Christian family who love the Lord. Their character reflects their faith in God. I was really ashamed throughout the service because I used to be their paper boy and I attended school with their daughters. Mr. Dickens reached out, grabbed both of my arms, and asked me, "How did you get so big like that, and how long have you been in prison?"

I expressed my passion for lifting weights during the four years in which I was incarcerated. Once we talked briefly, he questioned me about where I stood with the Lord and I told him that I wasn't ready to be committed. Then Mr. Dickens asked me, "Do you believe in Jesus, son?"

I said, "I don't fool with Jesus, and I don't believe in Him," not knowing that God was revealed in the person of Jesus Christ in the flesh.

Mr. Dickens asked me wisely, "Do you believe in God and read the Bible?"

I said, "Yes, sir."

Right before they left Mr. Dickens prayed with me and encouraged me to spend more time in my Bible. Then, Mr. Dickens told me boldly in front of his prison ministry team that God said He was going to supernaturally bless me out of prison real soon.

I had served four of the twenty-five years I had received. To me it was sort of hard to fully comprehend what Mr. Dickens had just told me, but I did sense a glimpse of hope within that something good was going to happen for me.

Two weeks after Mr. Dickens prophesied to me I got into a serious confrontation with another inmate named Gerald Johnson. We came to within seconds of a potential death by a knife fight because he retrieved my legal case out of the garbage can where I had thrown it away earlier that day. One of us was going to die and I was determined that it wasn't going to be Ma Jennie's baby boy.

There was a standoff between fifty-six men in Housing 6, Quad 4, with the young gladiators' generation on my side and the older gladiators' generation on Gerald's side. Half of these men were transferred with me from Sumter and stood with me. The other half were transferred with Gerald from Florida State Prison and stood with him. We got to the bottom of what created this intense confrontation and determined that it was sparked by acts of innocence on both of our parts.

I was a young blood, swollen from pumping iron, who extorted anybody who could be extorted. Gerald was a houseman, a junky for Mary J and more importantly, Gerald was Johnny Cochran in disguise. I didn't know that he was one of the best chain gang lawyers in prison. Gerald litigated my case in two weeks, and within thirty days I received a court order to be resentenced on October 26, 1986, in Panama City. Gerald's legal fees were half an ounce of Mary J and fifty dollars. Every legal word of counsel that Gerald instructed me to use in court was effective inasmuch as the scenarios he predicted came to pass.

During the first week of October, a sheriff's officer drove ten hours from Panama City to Martin County to take me back for my court proceeding. After a few court appearances and after going through their preliminary protocol with the judge, and state attorney, I exercised my legal rights and fired two different public pretending lawyers who were putting on the hits and playing with my freedom. That is, they acted as though they had my best interests at heart when that wasn't the case. Gerald had advised me that these pretending lawyers for the state would create this conflict of interest which would establish legal grounds for me to fire those two clowns.

In November 1986, the judge appointed me a private attorney. When the smoked cleared, the judge gave me time served with fifteen years' probation.

On January 15, 1987, the same transporting sheriff's officer drove me back to Martin County. Upon my return to the jungle at Martin C.I., Gerald and Ced expressed their excitement about the news that I was going home. Gerald's gifted skills as a paralegal were used to help get my freedom back.

Before I left Martin I got Gerald's and Ceds' DOC numbers so I could send them some money. I did so because no price compares to a man's freedom and genuine friendship.

Miraculously, six months after Mr. Dickens prophesied to me in that church service, I became a free man and walked out of Martin County C.I.!

ENDNOTES

1 Salvatore ("*Sammy the Bull*") Gravano was a former mobster who became underboss of the Gambino crime family. Salvatore became an informant for the New York State Attorney and testified against John Gotti ("*The Boss*").
2 Controlled, closed entryway to an enclosure.

Eleven

Ma Jennie's Baby Boy, Turk, is Home

THE NEXT DAY, January 16, 1987, I was called to the Visiting Park to be released back into society. The Visiting Park is the area where inmates visit with their loved ones on weekends. It is also the area from which inmates are released when returning home. I called Ma Jennie to come pick me up and she thought I was playing with her. She said, "Boy, I know you ain't calling my house bothering me while I am watching my favorite shows, *The Price is Right* and *All My Children* are getting ready to come on."

I had to get the classification officer to speak with her in order to convince her that I wasn't playing. He explained to her that Adam went back to outside court and they resentenced him, so he is free to go home. Twenty minutes later Ma Jennie and Loretta (*O.B.'s girlfriend*) drove up to take me home.

The first place I had them stop at was the Fernhill Cemetery so I could visit the gravesite of my daughter,

Amanda. As I walked back to the car where Mama and Loretta were waiting for me, two females hollered at me as they drove by. When I got back to Mama's car, I noticed a car nearby that contained the two females who had just passed by. Ma Jennie said, "This is your brother Duck's car; Sherry is his girlfriend and Tonya is her friend. They started tripping out that it was really me because they hadn't seen me in five years. They were really impressed by my well-defined, muscular body, dressed in a tank top and shorts. Upon my release, I was bench-pressing 385 lbs., inclining 315 lbs. and squatting 375 lbs. at the invincible age of 22. My body was seriously ripped with a balanced physique and a six pack to flex the total package.

Arriving back at Tarpon Ave. after five years, everything seemed so small. The first thing I noticed was that, where the pond used to be on East Lake Street and Tarpon, a new plaza had been built. Then, all of a sudden, I saw somebody running toward me at full speed. I didn't recognize him at first, but it was my cousin Michael Cooper. We embraced each other as we shared a few joyful tears.

I had the same experience with Duck. When he drove up in his car, he was really thrilled to see me. My coming home was a proud moment for Ma Jennie and the family. Mama's face was radiant to see that her baby boy was finally back home. Ma Jennie's front yard got crowded real fast as word got out that Turk was home.

Everyone was astonished at how swollen I was and was taking notice of the serious 22-inch python arms that

I was sporting. Then, James Long came into the yard and fired up a fat one that beamed me up to cloud nine. Out of nowhere, Mac, Jr. started his crazy laugh like a cartoonist's African laughing hyena. I became a little woozy and suddenly felt paranoid because too many people were crowding around and pulling on me. I was experiencing culture shock from having just stepped out of Florida's most violent, cut-throat danger zone at Martin CI.

Transitioning back into society was a humbling challenge for me. I told my cousin Mike to get me from around everybody. Right before I got into his car, Ma Jennie made me promise her that I wouldn't get into any trouble. Mike drove me around East Stuart in his Grand Prix sporting his Trues and Vogues (*combination of luxury tires and wheels*) with Jam Pony and 2 Live Crew booming from his sound system.

The next day I reported to my probation officer. It appeared to me that everyone in the building was anticipating my entrance, because as soon as I mentioned my name, heads peeped out of doors in the hallway.

My probation officer wanted to know my plan of action for staying out of prison. Doing so included how I was going to survive in a drug-infested neighborhood and in a drug-related dysfunctional family. He made sure that I was informed that almost everybody in my immediate family had a record, including Ma Jennie. Only Fred, Jennie Mae, Roxanne, Tiny, and Ski-Bo didn't have criminal records. He basically didn't give me a fighting chance to stay out long based upon my family's history with drugs.

My first Sunday home, Ma Jennie took me to Macedonia Baptist Church. She couldn't wait to tell Pastor Lewis that Turk was rejoining the church and joining the choir. I thought to myself, "Mama, stop talking so much. What do you mean, Turk is rejoining the church and choir?" Ma Jennie was officially welcoming me back to reality. Her words were still law, so I complied by rejoining the church and choir, but it was without a commitment to the Lord in my heart. Mrs. Johnson and the other church mothers assured me that they would be praying for me.

I attended church services and Bible studies often. I took up offerings for the sick and for the poor, I sang in the choir and even attended Southern Baptist Conventions with Pastor Lewis and his deacons. I did this all in the name of religion because I knew that I was a sinner who wasn't saved.

Pastor Lewis had to hear my thoughts because after one of his sermons, he pointed his finger at me and said, "God said He is calling you and if you don't repent and receive Jesus, you are going to HELL!" Immediately I thought, "Negro, God didn't tell you that. If God wanted me to know that, why didn't He tell me that Himself?" In my ignorance, those words really convicted, and scared me. Pastor Lewis had given me a license and excuse to drift away from the church.

Twelve

Ringing Like Southern Bell

PEOPLE IN THE know in the underground world on the Muck and in South Florida got word that my feet were back on the ground. My cousin Mike was already in my ear on day one trying to convince me to make it happen so we could set up shop. With no money in my pocket, I told Mike to chill as I was spending his money on every corner. Something had to give.

Because of my proven street and prison cred, Mike knew that it was just a matter of time before I set it off. In fact, he had a bigger itch than I did for me to set things in motion. A major trap had already been established where I was raised on Tarpon. It was for the taking with my brother Wine Head already in place to regulate things, but it wasn't the right time.

As the game and the nightclub life began to appeal more to me, I gradually got into the groove of things. One day I stopped by Johnny Bell's Barber Shop and Philip

Harvey hooked me up with a Jheri curl. I got my hair done in anticipation of a concert with an after party coming to Ft. Pierce, Florida, featuring rapper MC Shy-D of 2 Live Crew. Mike had four tickets and since I didn't have my own woman, I came up with someone else's woman for the weekend.

After the concert we went to Baker's which was a popular nightclub in Ft. Pierce. Standing at the bar with the ladies by our sides, a female walked by staring at me. She stopped to speak with Mike briefly as he nodded his head while looking at me.

A few minutes later the same female returned with another female. When their faces came into focus I realized it was Trina and her sister, Lil Moma. It was Trina, the mother of my daughter, the one who claimed that no other man could touch her with a ten-foot pole—yes, THAT Trina.

I just stared at her with a cold-blooded look. Crazy thoughts flashed through my mind as she explained why she was missing during my last five years of incarceration. When I refused her invitation to go to her house and see our daughter at 2:30 a.m., she asked me for a dance to Freddie Jackson's latest song, "Rock Me Tonight". Leaving my date at the bar, I gave Trina a three-minute dance of infatuated romance. While we danced, it was settled in my mind that it wasn't going down like that between us. That is, she definitely wasn't going to get rocked by me that night or any other night in the way Freddie was singing about.

The next day in Stuart, Trina brought our daughter Yashekia from Ft. Pierce to visit me. We had a wonderful time reacquainting ourselves. Though we lived thirty minutes apart, I still assumed my responsibility to support her in every aspect possible.

Renting cars and hotel rooms kept a hole in my pocket. I was tired of going in circles while my life wasn't going anywhere. I became frustrated and impatient for things to get better for me. Suddenly, my mind flashed back to the movie *Scarface* and its main character, Tony Montana. I decided to tell Mike and Wine Head that it was time to shut down my Aunt Pepper's and her Haitian husband's operation on Tarpon and take over.

I knew people who knew people who made things happen, which enabled me to cut back some serious flow. I really began to live a life of double standards between the streets, and the church (*where I didn't have a relationship with God*). I was caught up between the two with a false sense of direction.

The neighborhood's new bully was a very dangerous character named Roberto Daniels. He was a 230 lb. skillful martial arts fighter who was terrorizing Martin County drug dealers. When he heard about me, he made it his business to confront me on Tarpon with his extortion muscle game. Roberto didn't know that he was dealing with a certified extortioner straight up out of DOC. My tour of duty at Martin C.I. taught me how to take him out if he tried me. I told him point blank that, "I have heard how you kicked my cousin, Mike." I also said, "If you ever try me or harm anybody else in my family again, I promise you your whole family will be wearing black on Sunday just for you."

When he tried to reason with me I said, "Look man, I am living like that, I meant what I said and said what I meant—end of discussion." I never had one problem with Roberto as we conducted business together.

The next day at my probation meeting my counselor informed me that my name was ringing like southern bell (*Telephone company*) with a bad report. He advised me to clean up my act and get a legitimate job. That same week the Treasure Coast Job Training Center helped me get a job at an air conditioning and heating company. It was a good job but, unfortunately, they went out of business after I had been with them for five months. I then got a job at Stuart Toyota.

Meanwhile, on the side, I still maintained my own line of business in the hood. In the summer of 1987, my cousin Mike presented me with the idea of getting in on a deal with him and Cleve Brooks (*Mike's partner*) in a nightclub. Word was that Big Jack and Joe Harris (*older number runner and street hustler, respectively*) were going under financially. They didn't want us from a younger generation to get our hands on the nightclub. However, we had the flow they needed. Eventually, we came to the table, cut a deal with them and "The Pit" nightclub was established.

Despite negative press (*drug activity, crime, fights, shootings*), The Pit was a popular nightclub with an exciting buzz throughout the Treasure Coast area. The Pit was famous for its entertaining Gong Shows featuring Marty Hall (*singer and host of events*) and our very own popular singer Rodney Simpson.

In the summer of 1987 we started a traditional party scene on the Stuart Causeway beach by taking The Pit's sound system out there. After the beach, we headed back to Tarpon or the park with the music and crowd of people.

One day as I massaged Ma Jennie's shoulders and neck, she warned me to leave town for a while because of a dream she had concerning me. She advised me to visit her sister Sally Mae in Philadelphia. I took heed to her words of wisdom and, with the consent of my probation counselor, I was granted thirty days to enjoy my trip to Philadelphia.

That same day, I booked a flight to Philly which was scheduled to leave three weeks later, the second week of July. A week later a knock at my door woke me up at 4:00 a.m. It was my probation counselor with two detectives, one from Georgia and one from Tallahassee. They had questions for me concerning Harry Johnson's where-abouts because he had just escaped the prison system (DOC) with three life sentences, and he had committed several more robberies after his escape. I told them I hadn't seen him, which I hadn't, so they left after they concluded that I didn't have any information for them.

A few nights later I was in Baker's Nightclub in Ft. Pierce, packing with my nine when Sandra Jones from Hobe Sound approached me at the bar. I thought to myself, "Where is she coming from and what does she want with me?" Then, she whispered in my ear that Harry wanted to speak with me. I didn't know how he knew where I was, but I quickly decided to keep it real with him, knowing that there could be fatal consequences if I didn't do so.

I was a bit nervous as I followed Sandra out the door with one in the chamber of my nine on safety. We walked into an alley a few blocks over and there he was sitting in the back seat of a car in a dark alley. He was glad to see me but, unfortunately, I wasn't feeling the same way because of the circumstances. Here's a dangerous, desperate man on the run with his life on the line. He's fully armed like a Navy Seal ready for war, yet he took the time to ask me three questions with a request that I accomplish a favor for him. Specifically, he asked, "How are you doing? How are you living? Do you need any money?" I told him that I was doing well and doing my thang. Harry then told me that he had stashed some major flow in Tallahassee but because there was an all-out most wanted arrest warrant for him in three states, he was unable to retrieve that flow. He also told me that the next time he contacted me he would give me a map to the stash and instructions for what to do with it. Harry assured me that he was going to hold court on the street or wherever they ran down on him, because he was not going back to do another day in prison. After this secret meeting, we embraced and went our separate ways.

During the weekend of July 4, Ma Jennie questioned me about why I hadn't visited Sally Mae yet in Philadelphia. I assured her that I would be leaving for a month in a few days. The day before I was scheduled to fly out, I was driving out of Hobe Sound when Aaron Damn (*Bo-Dilly*) stopped me. He asked me if I heard what happened to Harry and I said "No." Bo-Dilly said it was just on TV that a State Trooper shot Harry in the head, killing him, after a traffic stop confrontation. This news spread like wildfire because Harry was raised in Hobe Sound and my name was associated with him from the robberies we committed in 1982. The news was a shocker even though he assured me that he was holding court in the streets. The shooting was anticipated but Harry was not expected to go out like that. Harry lived a lavish gangster lifestyle and died a violent death in vain — a desperate was man on the run for his life.

Thirteen

Flying High To South Philly

THE NEXT DAY I arrived at West Palm Beach International Airport, where I was scheduled to fly out on Delta Airlines. Before boarding the plane I went into the nearest restroom to be alone with Mary J. I wanted to be high before I reached the sky in the event the plane went down, so my demise would be swift and painless.

In two hours and thirty minutes I was landing in South Philadelphia, the "City of Brotherly Love". I called Aunt Sally Mae from the airport before I caught a cab to let her know I was in Philly. She was so happy to see me because I used to call her collect when I was in prison and I promised her that I would visit her when I came home.'

Upon arriving at 18th and Washington, in front of Aunt Sally's house, I heard a man's voice from across the street yell out, "Hey, who are you looking for?"

When I looked to see where this voice came from, I recognized his older face and asked, "Is that you Uncle Andrew?"

He responded, "Who in the Hell are you?" I beat him to the punch by selling him out first, but this fool took things to a whole other level by upping his gun and starting to cuss me out ferociously.

Immediately I started calling, "Sally Mae, Sally Mae," and he said "Don't be calling Sally Mae now, you son-of-a-.....!"

When Sally Mae came to the door looking just like Ma Jennie's twin, she yelled at Andrew to put up the gun and took me inside the house. Once he calmed down, he came inside and started telling me that he ain't going to have no jailbird in his house.

Then Sally jumped in and said, "This is my house and you don't run anything but your mouth." This was a classic couple carrying on just like Redd Foxx and Esther on Sanford and Son. They both were funny in a loving way.

When I peeped that she could handle him, I really started throwing gasoline on him with trash talk. Upon realizing that Sally had my back as we were laughing at him, he flipped the script on us. Now he wanted to know what I went to prison for and how I survived with a pretty face and a Jheri curl.

I came back at Andrew by telling him that in prison he would have been paying me for protection.

After Sally and I tag teamed and beat him at his own game, he got serious and said, "I don't care how slick you talk, you have to earn your keep in order to sleep in this house."

On that note, Sally agreed with Andrew that I had to help him remodel their house across the street to rent out.

With his whiskey in hand, I followed him across the street and he instructed me on what he wanted me to do. While I worked, this joker was sipping on his whiskey and telling South Philly jokes.

After working a few hours, I noticed that Andrew had gotten really tipsy, so I hit him with a few DOC jokes which didn't even faze him. I had to hit him with something that would strike one of his nerves, so I said "Listen man, I didn't come to Philadelphia for your raggedy self to slave-drive me in your junkyard funky house!"

He stared at me with a crazy alcoholic look while sipping on his whiskey bottle, which indicated to me that those words hit something as they sunk into his mind. After a few seconds, he upped his gun again and said, "You got all them damn muscles but you are the sorriest piece of manure that I ever saw in South Philly."

I knew that he wasn't going to shoot me. At least I was hoping he wouldn't shoot me. So, I popped off some more, like I didn't even see him or his gun, but God knows I did see that .357 Magnum in that fool's hand. Then, Andrew got really messed up when I pulled out a bag of Mary J, rolled it up, licked it, fired it up and passed it to him while he continued holding me at gunpoint.

When he saw this, he started calling Sally Mae as he left me smoking Mary J. A few minutes later I heard Sally calling for me. After I got myself together, I went inside where he was telling her that "This boy really don't have good sense; that prison time he did has messed his mind up and ruined his life." Then he asked me, "How long are you going to stay in Philly?"

When I replied "thirty days" homeboy really took off. After he settled down, he offered me a drink of his whiskey, but it was a little strong for me, so I passed on his offer.

He then started joking that my weak stomach and jelly backbone couldn't hold his whiskey. When I tried to come back at him with a joke, he upped his gun again, but this time Sally Mae snatched it out of his hand. That got him off me and he started clowning on Aunt Sally Mae, which turned out to be a special and hilarious comedic moment.

During my first night in Philly, I called Rudolph back in Florida to get his people's number who lived in West Philly. Rudy was like, "Bro, where are you?"

"South Philly."

"Yea, right."

"Straight up man, I am in South Philly chilling. What's up?"

"Man, people are tripping because Harry just got killed and you aren't anywhere to be found, with people looking for you."

I told Rudy to keep this information close to the vest and not have loose lips revealing my whereabouts to the haters and nosy crowd. Rudolph just laughed and said Boy you are something else." After he gave me the phone number, he hung up and I called his people to find out how to get to the West Side by the buses and trolleys.

The Jamison family was surprised to see me in West Philly by myself. The first thing they said was, That's Ma Jennie's boy, Turkey Red." They wanted to talk about the latest gossip on how they said I had it going on in South Florida. I quickly downplayed whatever report they received, to get the focus off me.

Once I learned my way around the City of Brotherly Love, I had fun at the Plato Park and downtown center where people shop and hang out. Since Luther Vandross was in town, I caught him live at the Spectrum basketball arena.

One day while sitting outside Aunt Sally's house I thought I saw a familiar face getting out of a car next door. It was Karen, a longtime childhood friend I used to play with in the snow years prior, in the early seventies.

After we caught up on each other's past and present statuses, she offered to catch a movie with me and show me the town. Uncle Andrew was ear hustling and couldn't wait to ask me, "How many lies did you tell her?" I didn't feed his madness because I had a date to catch and enjoy.

Karen and I caught the freshly released movie, *Predator*. While we chatted in line waiting to buy our popcorn and Cokes, she noted that everyone in the lobby had picked up on my Southern accent. It was a really big deal for them to hear my Southern vernacular in the City of Brotherly Love. After the movie, she showed me the town and where to buy the latest fashionwear. Before I left Philly, I bought the latest gear that I knew wasn't in South Florida.

My thirty days had come to pass and I had to hear my last earful from Andrew and receive my last sweet words from Aunt Sally Mae. I embraced Pretty Sally for the last time as I expressed my love to her. Then, I gave my Uncle Andrew a chest bump with a strong handshake and a few slick words before I got into the cab to leave Philly.

As I checked my bags in the airport, a few men approached me about drugs when they caught my accent. First, they thought that I played ball and then they asked me if I was from the South. Either they really wanted some drugs or they were undercover police. It didn't matter because I only had a personal stash for myself. In fact, it was time for me to be alone with Mary J before I flew high.

Fourteen

You Think You're a Gangster

THANK GOD WE arrived safe and sound back at Palm Beach International Airport.

On September 11, 1987, I turned twenty-three and felt lucky, so I played 523 on a Cash 3 (*lottery ticket*) that I bought at Publix. It was a really special day because I hit and won $500.

One night at the Pit Nightclub the police found two ounces of crack cocaine. When they left, I got word that they were coming back with a fake warrant so they could take me in to the station. Before they returned, I had left town to head for the Muck, "doing the dashboard" (*traveling 90 to 100 MPH*) in my white and blue ragtop Cutlass.

The next day, I met Mike and Cleve at the West Palm Beach auditorium at 7:30 p.m. where Heavy D. and New Edition were live in concert. After having a great time at the concert, I discovered, painfully, that somebody had performed a Houdini act and stolen my baby. I'm talking about my pretty white and blue ragtop car—that baby!

As Mike and Cleve walked to the sections where our cars were parked, I started looking crazy. When I told them that my car had been stolen, it sounded like a joke to them. Then Cleve said sarcastically, "Dirty, you need to lay off that powder," and he drove off as I started to pop off, cussing him and Mike out.

Shortly after that the police drove up and I started popping off on them because they weren't on their job preventing my car from being stolen.

The theft of my popular car became an instant hot topic in East Stuart with the haters and imitators. Even certain police in Stuart stopped by in the hood to express their fake concern.

Two weeks later I bounced back with a clean 1982 two-toned brown Grand Prix with "30s-N-Lows" (*special expensive tires and rims*). That car had an earthshaking sound system that "put everybody on the door" (*meaning that no one could compete with me*) in the Treasure Coast area. One can hear the sounds of Maze featuring Frankie Beverly live in New Orleans coming out of that booming sound system.

I thought I had a sure lock to win big on John Elway and his Broncos against Doug Williams and his Redskins in the 1987 Super Bowl game. Taking all the bets at the Pit Nightclub, I lost big time. During the third quarter, I paid everyone their money and pumped up the music as we watched the rest of the game on the big screen TV.

It was my season of bad luck because the next week I was arrested on drug charges.

After I regrouped from a few setbacks, I bought a 1969 Mercedes. I restored it with a fresh maroon master paint job and dropped some "50s-N-Lows" (*expensive rims and tires*) on it. It was a sight of classic beauty.

Around this same period of time an anonymous admirer was surveilling my swag. Late one night I heard a car stop in front of my apartment and as I looked through my window, I saw someone leaning over the front windshield of my Mercedes.

When I went outside, I saw a car speeding off, so I quickly began pursuing the car to finally identify the potential admirer or serious stalker. As I drove back to my apartment in my Grand Prix, I noticed that an envelope had been placed under the windshield wiper on my Mercedes. The card inside the envelope said . . . well, I can't tell you what she said to me in the card, but I will tell you that she signed it "your secret admirer."

One of the survival skills I perfected while doing time at Sumter and at Martin was how to set traps for intended victims. Wisely, I set a human trap like a trap set with cheese for catching a rat. I caught the secret admirer just like that—like a rat that sees the cheese but doesn't see the trap.

I trapped her in a traffic jam in the hood on East Lake Street between Nassau and Bahama Avenues beside a car wash. When she tried to slide through the hood to sweat my swag on the sly, I pulled my car directly in front of hers while a truck boxed her in from behind. She was totally surprised as I rushed to the driver's side of her car and snatched the keys out of the ignition.

I interrogated her on the spot until she finally came clean and admitted that she was the secret admirer. Upon that admission, I gave her back her car keys. It came to pass eventually that I finally gave her what she wanted and we started something between us.

Shortly after this episode, a familiar car with tinted windows drove up and stopped in front of Ma Jennie's house. When the windows rolled down on the driver's side, I recognized that the driver was Julio with five of his nieces. I asked him what he wanted and he said, "My niece Esther has a crush on you and I wanted to introduce her to you personally."

I said to Julio, "Man are you tripping? You better get your niece up off Tarpon." That didn't stop Esther from talking to me.

One afternoon I went to Mike's parents' house with him not knowing that a surprise confrontation awaited me.

Esther and her grandmother, Mrs. Kamala, were standing outside their house directly across the street waiting for me to come out of Mike's parents' house. When we came outside to get into Mike's car to leave, Mrs. Kamala said, "Hey you." When Mike responded to her, she said, "I'm not talking to you Mike, I'm talking to him."

I said, "Me?"

She said, "Yes, you."

"Yes Ma'am."

"You think you are bad, don't you?" I heard about you. You think that you're a gangster?"

As I stood by Mike's car while she was talking smack, I popped off and said, "Lady, you don't know me—Mike, this old lady is tripping man, let's go." Obviously, I had struck a nerve with her because she really took off talking trash to me inside their fenced yard.

Mike started laughing as she told me to come see what she wanted. I honestly didn't want anything to do with this slick talking lady or her beautiful, young granddaughter. Out of respect for her Mike said, "Man just go see what she wants so we can go." Since Mike put me on the spot, I walked across the street to see what she wanted.

While Esther stood there beside her looking all pretty and innocent, Mrs. Kamala said with a threatening demeanor, "Negro, what have you done to my daughter?"

"Nothing."

"Don't you lie to me."

I was really trying to be respectful to her, so I said, "The last time I checked it wasn't a crime to talk with someone in Martin County."

After she popped off a few more words of her disapproval of me seeing or talking to Esther, she said that her husband wanted to talk with me. I told her point blank, "I don't want to talk with your husband."

Mrs. Kamala said, "Boy you really don't have good sense for real, do you?" I didn't want to get radical with her, so I rolled with the flow and spoke with her husband, Mr. Albert (Al), Esther's grandfather.

Upon entering their house, I saw Al sitting at the kitchen table like he was the godfather or somebody to be feared. Once he asked me to have a seat, he said "So you are Ma Jennie's boy who has my daughter's attention. Esther has told me that she really likes you and if she likes you, I like you." Meanwhile Mrs. Kamala was standing behind Al looking at me with the sharpness of an eagle's eye. Al said, "Me and my wife have discussed this and I have decided to allow Esther to see you."

With Esther sitting by his side looking at me teary eyed, Al said, "Let me explain something to you, Esther is my only daughter that I have raised; I love her with all my heart and there's nothing that I won't do for her." Then he looked at me with his bloodshot red eyes across from the table and said, If you ever hit Esther or mistreat her, Negro, I will kill you."

Hearing Al's words really didn't sit well with me. This skinny Black joker wasn't even big in stature, so I popped off immediately telling him that he didn't know who he was messing with. Simultaneously as I stood up, Mrs. Kamala came at me saying, "You ain't no gangster and you ain't going to be talking to my husband like that either," as she nudged me upside my head. Meanwhile, Al had stood up and was digging in his Dickies' work pants' pocket faking like he was reaching for a gun.

From my prison experience, I sensed that he was bluffing while putting on the hits. For one, he was stuttering when he threatened me; two, he was talking too much, like a junkyard dog that was barking though he knew he wasn't going to harm anybody. My senses and experience served me right because when Al did pull his hands out of his pocket, this joker was holding a handful of screws, washers and spark plugs for his lawn mowers. Al pump faked harder than Bret Favre. Though he didn't pull one of his raggedy guns on me, I understood his concern as he approved of Esther having a relationship with me. While Mrs. Kamala observed from the kitchen table, her look spoke volumes.

Fifteen

She Was Going to Kill Me

DURING SPRING BREAK 1988, I took DJ Red with me to Daytona Beach to do what people do over Spring Break. It was my first time there and Daytona Beach lived up to the hype with its clubs and party scenes. It was definitely the place to be to have a really great time with some high energy fun.

A week before I turned myself in to serve an eighteen-month prison sentence for sells of drugs, I bought my mother a Cadillac Coupe. I delivered it to her at her job at Glades General Hospital in Belle Glade. She was totally shocked and surprised because at first, she thought it was one of her supervisor's cars. When I showed her the paperwork with Jennie Mae Jolly's name on it, she cried with joy because she never owned a car. It was a touching moment for her because Glades General is the same place where she birthed me, and her baby was delivering her the desire of her heart at his birthplace. Before leaving Belle

Glade, I stopped by to see Cool Breeze (*my dad*) so I could give him a fresh new pair of leather Dr. J's.

Cool Breeze said, "Adam, how much do these shoes cost?"

I told him, "Ninety dollars."

He screamed, "Jesus Christ, son you are crazy! I could have bought ten pair of shoes from Winn Dixie." Cool Breeze was referring to buying Cat Head tennis shoes. My dad is an original throwback from Nassau, Bahamas, so he is really "El Cheapo" when it comes to spending money for quality things.

At 3 a.m. my phone rang. It was Jennie Mae. I asked, "Mama, is everything okay?" She said, "Baby, I am still riding the town in my new car. My friends and coworkers think that I have won the lotto. Mama loves you and thank you baby."

I had to turn myself in to the prison system the morning of July 29, 1988. Normally, one would have to serve at least twelve months of an eighteen-month sentence. However, that same week I arrived at Lake Butler Reception Center, a new incentive gain time system was established because of the overcrowding in the prison system.

I was transferred to Berry Dale Forest Work Camp in Jay, Florida, which is a ten-hour drive from Martin County. My cousins Mike and Steve visited me on my birthday, September 11, and I informed them of my possible early release situation.

On November 2, 1988, just after serving 93 days, I was informed that my time was completed and I could go home. I was driven to Pensacola's bus station and rode a bus to the Tallahassee bus station on Tennessee Street. Once I got there, I called Mike to come pick me up because I didn't want to be on a bus to South Florida for another five hours.

In four-and-a-half hours, Mike and Julio drove up onto Tennessee Street to get me and we cruised back to South Florida.

Two weeks later on November 17, 1988, I personally witnessed Candee Marie Jolly come into this world.

The next day Mike called me on my shoe-sized Motorola cell phone as I was rolling in my Mercedes. Mike informed me that people in the underground world in the Dirty South wanted to make it happen for us. I told him, "I'm bringing my flow for you to handle that because I have to sign for my baby today and I can't go." He then told me that somebody had broken his brother Steve's jaw at Florida Memorial College in South Florida, where Steve was a student.

Two hours later, I found myself in Miami with Mike on Florida Memorial College's campus to see about Steve. We were unable to run down on the cowards who jumped

Steve, so we handled our drug business and headed north on I-95.

On our way back on the Florida turnpike in a 1978 Seville with 50s-N-Lows and a rag top, we got knocked off for trafficking cocaine in Palm Beach County.

My whole world came crashing down on me. I couldn't believe it was going down like that before my eyes. I felt miserable and doomed with a lump in my throat that made me feel like not talking to anybody. It was mandatory that I dial up a master plan to come up out of the Gun Club County Jail in West Palm Beach.

My cousin Carmen, Mike's sister, visited us to encourage us that everything would be all right. Then she pleaded with Mike and me to stop the drug business. Carmen asked us, "What are y'all trying to prove and what more are y'all trying to accomplish? The families are very disturbed, and on pins and needles, because of you two."

She was saying some sobering and encouraging words, but while she was talking I was thinking about my next move. Mike and I hired Nelson Bailey, a prominent attorney.

In February 1989, I had to serve thirty days in the Martin County Jail for a misdemeanor. While serving this time, an officer informed me that some female wanted me to call her ASAP because she had some very important news for me. The secret admirer had me under surveillance until I trapped her.

When I called her, she answered the phone crying and I told her I didn't call her to hear any drama. She said, When you get out, I have something at my parents' house that belongs to you which you need to come see."

I told her, "I haven't left anything at your parents' house."

That's when she dropped a bomb on me by saying that she birthed our son Jeremiah on January 10, 1989.

Upon getting out early to attend Mrs. Mini Will Jacob's funeral, I stopped by her parents' house. Her grandmother was sitting in a wheelchair in the kitchen and she said, "Bring that baby here to me." When she brought the baby to her, she said to me, "Young man come closer to me so that I can see you real good." Then, looking at the baby in her arms and looking at me, she said, "This is the baby daddy right here, and not that other boy."

I was truly fortunate to be attending Mrs. Mini Will's funeral and not mine. Because of the multiple females I was involved with, anything was subject to pop off at any given moment.

Mrs. Mini Will was an elderly lady who was well known in the community, who still dressed eloquently in her own jazzy style. We became very close after I stopped her husband Johnny from jumping on her. After the first and fifteenth of each month, when they were drunk and broke, some serious cussing and ugly fighting would be going down between them. One day in front of Ma Jennie's house, Johnny was pushing and hitting Mini Will as he cussed her out. That's when I stepped in to stop him by jacking him up. Johnny said, Man what's wrong with you, that's my woman." I told him that he wasn't going to be jumping on her in front of me.

When Mini Will saw that Johnny respected me, she really got bad as she stood behind me cussing Johnny out with boldness. From that day forward she began to tell Johnny that "Turk is my man now and he ain't going to let you hit me."

Often, early in the morning, Ma Jennie would call me to come get Mini Will out of her house because Johnny was outside waiting to jump on her. When I would drive up, Mini Will would come out of Ma Jennie's house cussing Johnny out and telling him, "Here comes my man, now bring it on with your bad self. Turk and I going to kick your butt." I was twenty-four and they were in their early seventies, so you can imagine the scene with the neighborhood winos across the street yelling and telling Johnny, "Turk has taken your woman."

Unfortunately, one day Mrs. Mini Will had a pretty bad stroke and the only person's name she would call was "Turk". One of her daughters, Mrs. Lee Jacobs (a *Stuart police officer*), stopped by Ma Jennie's house to let me know that her mother wanted to see me. When I built up my nerve, I went to visit my friend in her unpleasant situation. It really humbled and touched me to see her like that, and all she mumbled was "Turk, Turk, Turk." As I felt helpless with her alone, I just hugged her as she shed uncontrollable tears. Before I left her, I kissed Mrs. Mini Will on her twisted jaw and told her I loved her. That was my last time seeing her alive before I went to jail for the misdemeanor.

Her daughter, Mrs. Lee Jacob, requested of the Jail Warden that I be released early so I could attend her mother's funeral at Mt. Calvary Church.

While we were out on bail for trafficking, Mike was busted again on more drug charges. This caused his dad to have a heart attack, and guess who was made out to be the bad guy—Turk. One of Mike's sisters, Beatrice, drove up on Tarpon unexpectedly to tell me personally that if her daddy died in the hospital, she was going to kill me. She didn't even give me a chance to say I didn't have anything to do with what Mike did. As she drove off, I said, "Now she's supposed to be a Christian . . . and she's my cousin."

I think she heard me because thirty minutes later one of Mike's other sisters drove up and said, "Turk, Beatrice wants you to come to her house." Mike had eight sisters and one brother, which really caused me to not want to go to her house. I thought about taking my gun but this was family, so I had to take it like a man if they decided to jump me about their father.

Having seen all their cars in the yard, I took a deep breath before I entered Beatrice's house. I took only one step inside the door in case I had to make an emergency exit. As I surveyed the living room carefully, all teary eyes were fixed on me as Beatrice stood to apologize for threatening to kill me. Though she toned it down a little, it was obvious that her disposition toward me hadn't changed as she gave it to me concerning how they were all feeling about their father.

Beatrice then asked me, "Aren't you tired of selling that poison to people?"

In my mind I said "No," as I stood before them, looking as though I hadn't heard the question. With tears in her eyes, she pleaded with me to stop selling drugs. But her words and tears didn't even faze or move me. I just said "Okay," took one step back and I was out the door. Thank God their father pulled through because I didn't want to resort to my Martin C.I. survival tactics to protect myself.

When their father got better, I started changing more of Candee's diapers and going to church. Going to church always gave Mrs. Johnson and Mrs. Janie an opportunity to pray for me because they knew I wasn't living right.

The secret admirer brought the baby around on Tarpon a few times, but she decided wisely to allow her ex-boyfriend and his parents to raise him because of the direction in which my life was headed.

One day I woke up and decided to trade both of my cars for a Chevy Blazer. Then, I bought a jet ski so I could ride at the beach whenever I so desired. Mike and Cleve bought jet skis also and the three of us would spend time barbequing, jamming out with music, and riding on the water at the Stuart Causeway.

We made the Stuart Causeway the popular place to be during the summer and every other weekend. I enjoyed giving the neighborhood kids rides on my jet ski. I also enjoyed playing the latest music in all the parks, clubs, block parties, pool parties, and house parties in Martin County.

Though I lived a criminal lifestyle, I gave back to the needy and less fortunate in East Stuart.

I took Cleve and Steve with me to Daytona Beach during Spring Break 1989. Daytona Beach was definitely the place to be during spring break if you were looking for a great time and an all-night partying atmosphere. It takes flow to do what we did to make things happen at Daytona Beach. Only true ballers knew how to make things happen while the spectators, imitators, and the haters watched things happen.

Sixteen

Lord, Don't Let the Devil Kill My Boy

ARRIVING BACK IN East Stuart, my homeboy Freddie Wiley asked me for a favor on the come up (*making money selling drugs*). Later that afternoon, I took him on a mission to the underground world in West Palm Beach. When we rolled up on a certain trap (*drug spot*), a murder had just gone down and the scene was chaotic with every hustler packing some serious artillery. I was advised that the trap was shut down and was told to get off the set because a potential crossfire was subject to pop off any second.

In the midst of this madness, before Freddie and I left, we cut a deal hastily with an unfamiliar baller. One hour later, we both discovered to our surprise, that we had been robbed of several stacks (*thousands*) without a gun. It was painful, but we had to swallow this bad deal and charge it to the game which was the hustler's code. However, I realized four months' later that I hadn't swallowed that loss completely. Standing on Tarpon while cutting back some serious flow (*money was coming in every second*), a killing demon which I recognized from my time at Martin C.I., whispered in my ear for me to Go to West Palm and kill that joker who robbed you and Freddie; he is hustling in that same trap right now."

Then my partner who was also one of my classmates, Marvin Parks, said "What's up Dirty?"

I said, "Nothing man."

With a my mind made up to go on an assassination mission, I packed my Nine, and as I got into the car Marvin jumped in on the passenger side. Under the influence of powdered cocaine, Mary J, and Hennessey, it was on as we headed down I-95 South.

When Marvin asked me what the deal was, I simply told him that I was going to West Palm to kill the joker who robbed me and Freddie four months prior. He said, "Let's do it Dirty."

Marvin and I pulled up at the same trap with my Nine under my shirt, and we got out of the car. I knew the ballers who controlled this trap, so I explained to them what went down since it happened in their spot. I gave them the option to fix what went down to keep the peace or I was going to do what I came to do. With the kiss of death looming over their heads, they deceived me into thinking that they were going to make things right by fixing my flow to keep the peace.

After a few minutes of thinking that everything was cool, I sent Marvin inside a local store to buy us two cold Heinekens. When he came back, we sat in the car to chill and for some reason I decided to put the gun under the seat. Then, as soon as we stepped outside of the car *without my gun*, the joker who was the victim I intended to kill seemingly beamed down out of nowhere like in Star Trek. He had the drop on me (*I couldn't do anything as I was a sitting duck*). Suddenly, it was obvious to me that it was a double cross. Standing directly in front of me, about ten yards away, he pointed his semi-automatic hand gun at my chest and said, "Word is you told my boyz that you are here to wet me up (*euphemism for killing someone*)."

This deadly set up really blew my high when the scene went into slow motion as the barrel of his gun became larger than it really was. I was on the very edge of losing control of my bowels. My entire life flashed through my mind as well as the Godly prayers of church mothers at Macedonia Church. During that moment of time in the face of death, I heard Ma Jennie's voice saying clearly, "Lord, don't let that Devil kill my boy."

The next voice I heard was that of the fool with the gun. He said, "I'm going to kill him first," referring to Marvin who was sitting on the hood of the car five feet to my right. I thought to myself, "Lord, no! Please don't let this fool kill Marvin." At that point I had settled in my mind that if he pulled the trigger, I was going all in and out Martin C.I. style. Then it seemed like he heard my thoughts because he pointed the gun back at me and told everyone standing nearby to clear out.

My last plea was, "Lord, please don't let this Negro pull the trigger because I don't want to die like this." While he continued talking, my experience from Sumter and Martin kicked in. Don't panic or make any sudden moves because, like a barking dog isn't going to bite anybody, a talking joker isn't going to bust a grape. That is, he wasn't going to pull the trigger.

After a few minutes of war words, he slowly backed away from us with his gun pointed in our direction. As

I began to inch toward the car to get my Nine, one of the bystanders who had our best interests at heart said, "Be still my man and look behind that street pole." Because I was totally focused on the fool with the gun, I didn't see his reinforcement posted up thirty yards away with an AK-47 assault rifle beaming down on Marvin and me.

As they both ran off without firing a shot, we quickly got into the car to pursue them, then the thought occurred to me that one of these fools had an AK-47 which could rip holes easily through the car and us like Swiss cheese.

While this brief pursuit took place, Marvin and I were hyperventilating and cussing at each other. Then, the very moment I stopped pursuing these thugs, Marvin really started flipping out and saying that he was going to kill me for almost getting him killed.

At that moment, a ruthless scene out of the movie *Scarface* came to mind. Specifically, the scene in which Tony Montana blew away Sosa the hit man who was on the passenger side of the car talking crazy just like Marvin. He was definitely in the wrong position talking about killing Ma Jennie's boy when I was the only one who had a gun in the car.

Knowing that Marvin's mother was a devout Christian, it had to be her prayers that prevented me from whacking him. I drove home in silence as I endured Marvin's verbal abuse until he got tired of talking. Then this joker asked me, "Where's the ye yo [powdered cocaine], Dirty?" The whole time he didn't understand that his mother's prayers had him covered from the monster that was on the inside of me.

Two weeks later I found myself between my cousin Curl and Ma Jennie's word of prophecy that came to pass tragically. Curl and Duck were being disrespectful in Ma Jennie's house and she told them to leave, but Curl refused to leave as Duck left him talking trash to Ma Jennie. She told Curl to leave one more time, but this time Curl said, "You can't make me go nowhere."

The next thing I knew, Ma Jennie was pointing her judgment finger at Curl. I stumbled out of the way of her pointed finger because I knew what that signified in our culture. Pointing directly at Curl, Ma Jennie said, "You won't live to see twenty-one."

Two months later, Curl was shot three times in front of the Cherokee Motel. I was the last person who talked with Curl as he lay on the ground in a dark alley. With three holes in his body as a multitude of people crowded around, I had to convince Curl to allow the paramedics to give him some oxygen and get him to the hospital because he was running out of time and air; he was running out of life.

Three hours later at 3:45 a.m. on October 12, 1989, Kelvin Preston (*Curl*) was pronounced dead at Martin Memorial Hospital. As with death in any family, Curl's death united families and friends together from near and far to pay their respects to the deceased.

The next weekend Mike, Cleve, DJ Red, and I rolled up to Atlanta, Georgia for a weekend. We rolled with other ballers out of Miami and Ft. Lauderdale, enjoying the City of Atlanta. Before leaving we hung out downtown on Peachtree Street and caught Patti LaBelle and Tony Toni Tone live in concert at the amphitheater.

On our way back home we stopped on the Southside of Jacksonville, Florida to surprise my Prison Gladiator partner, Cedrick Vernon. Ced was at work release and was surprised and glad to see me. I broke him off (*gave him some money*) before I left him.

After being out on bond for a year, on November 30, 1989, Mike and I reported to the Palm Beach County Courthouse to be sentenced for drug trafficking charges. Our attorney, Nelson Bailey, cut a deal for me to receive a year and a day, and for Mike to receive six years.

Of the year-and-a-day I received, I served only fifty-three days, at the Henry C.I. Six hours after I was released as a free man, there was a statewide warrant for my arrest. I had thirteen more days to do for a Disciplinary Report (*D.R.*) I got for getting caught with $100 I wasn't supposed to have in my possession. The next morning my phone rang at my apartment. It was the head of the Classification Department at Henry C.I. He pleaded with me to turn myself in to help save his job because he was the one who was responsible for signing the paperwork for my release. I talked trash to him before we reasoned and then I gave him my word that I would bring myself back personally to Henry by 5:00 p.m.

I wanted to see my hero, Ma Jennie, before leaving. While driving in East Stuart, a police officer recognized me behind the wheel. Before I knew it, several police cars pursued and tried to stop me, so I decided, wisely, to drive on to the police station.

I got out of the car with my hands on my head as the police had their guns drawn. Once inside, I convinced the Chief of Police to call Henry C.I. to speak with the head of the Classification Department. After their lengthy discussion, they finally released me so that I could drive myself back to prison. After I visited Ma Jennie briefly, it took me one hour and forty-five minutes to drive to Henry C.I.

Two weeks later, in the month of January 1990, I was officially a free man, again.

During this season of my life, I couldn't explain it, but on the inside of me a force was driving and influencing my thoughts and actions. I thought that I was really living, but in reality I was chasing a deceptive mirage as my life was wasting away physically and I was dying spiritually. I thought I was balling but the sad truth was that I couldn't see I was falling.

Because of the various promiscuous relationships I was involved in, I was experiencing some turbulent backlash. It was what it was, so I had to deal with it accordingly and it wasn't always pretty. To magnify the drama, my weed head Aunt Mary Ann had some hot information concerning my females' business and she held it against me to bribe me into supporting her habit. She took it too far for me one day, so I had to show her that her nephew really didn't care what she said because I was just going to lie my way out of it anyway. I learned that from Harry Hippy (*O.B.'s gangster friend*). Harry said, "Turk, only tell a lie when it benefits you the most and don't tell one just for the hell of it."

When Mary Ann realized that she couldn't blackmail me anymore, she told me that she was going to take out a good insurance policy on me. She said, "When one of these girls kill you, I will be able to collect a big check." In her own words, to rub it in, she said "Child please."

One day, on Tarpon Ave., Kim told me that Lil Joe was behind the Browns' building crying with a gun in his hands, saying he was going to kill Turk. Earlier, Lil Joe and I exchanged words because I wouldn't serve him so he tried to lure me into an alley to take me out. What he didn't know was, Ma Jennie had prayed, "Lord, don't let the Devil kill my boy."

Seventeen

Baby, When are You Going to Stop Selling that Stuff?

ONE DAY AFTER church service at Macedonia, Mrs. Louise ("*Weezie*") Matheny had someone standing outside with a message for Ma Jennie's boy. She wanted me to come to her house after church. I didn't have any idea what she wanted and I really didn't want to go by her house. To be sure that I got her message, she had sent two different messengers.

Mrs. Matheny was a sweet loving elderly mother who attended St. Paul A.M.E. Church in East Stuart. I knew I had to go by and see her or I would be hearing from her again until I did stop by. I tried to ease by her house hoping she wouldn't be sitting on her porch under her big tree, but there she was sitting there waiting for me.

Mrs. Matheny said, "Baby, get out that truck and come see what I want." When I walked up to her porch she said, "Baby, you sure look like Willie Jerry (*my Uncle, O.B.*) when he was your age. You are a fine dressing, good-looking young man. Come on over here and sit by Mama for a while." Then she said, "I heard you be going to church sometimes and that's always the right place to be. I know Ma Jennie raised all her boys the best she could 'round there. That's why I wanted to talk with you." Mrs. Matheny then said, "Baby, when are you going to stop selling that stuff? Don't you know you are killing people with that poison?"

I couldn't do anything but look at her because she was holding my hands as she talked to me. Then she called for her youngest daughter, Delores, to bring us some tea to drink while we sat on the porch under her tree. Delores really didn't care for me, I guess because of my lifestyle. It was her right to hate. Whatever her issue was with me, she still brought Mama and me that cold sweet tea and it was good. The way she was looking at her mother was like, "What in the world do you see in this no-good drug dealer?"

Before I left, Mrs. Matheny asked me again, "Baby, when are you going to stop selling that stuff?"

Looking into her loving and caring eyes, I said, "Mama just pray for me." She wisely prayed with me that the Lord would watch over me, keeping me from all hurt, harm, and danger. Then she asked God to grant me His free gift of salvation and not allow the Devil to destroy my life. After praying with me, she would always end her prayer "In Jesus' name."

Mrs. Matheny made sure she always shared with me about the Lord Jesus and why He came. She would hold my hand in her hand when she talked with me so I had to hear it. During our first conversation, I gave her my word that I would stop by when I do go to church. She also asked me to bring her the Sunday Stuart newspaper, which was her way of getting me to stop by.

During the summer of 1990 I was looking at Ma Jennie's house (*the one I was raised in*) and decided to remodel it from top to bottom, inside and outside. I had to convince Ma Jennie into going to Philadelphia first because I knew she didn't want to go. After I bought her plane ticket to stay in Philly for thirty days, I had Fred and Tiny drive her to the airport in West Palm to fly her out. As soon as they pulled off Tarpon, I hired the neighborhood's skillful carpenters, roofers, plumbers, and tile layers.

Ma Jennie's baby boy gave her house a makeover with a seven-foot fence around it. She now had air conditioning with ceiling fans, new sofas, and a new reclining chair from which to watch Bob Barker on *"The Price if Right,"* and *"All My Children."*

Arriving back home after thirty days in Philadelphia, she got out of the car and everybody was waiting for her response concerning her remodeled house. As Ma Jennie stood in silence looking amazed with both hands on her hips, one of the winos across the street yelled out, "Hey Ma Jennie, why you let Turk put you in jail behind that big fence?" Then as she went inside she said, "Where is my record player, bar?" Wine said, "Turk threw them away."

When we walked into the kitchen she said, "Where are my damn wedding and anniversary glass cups?" Simultaneously as Wine Head said, "Turk threw them away too," the back of Mama's right hand came too fast at my face for me to move out of the way. She caught me between my nose and mouth as I moved swiftly out of striking range. Mama said, "Don't you run from me." I said, "Mama, I am sorry" as I backtracked out of the house.

I didn't realize that those dull-looking old glass cups had sentimental value concerning her marriage and anniversaries with Mr. Henry. As time passed, she forgave me with her kind words of love. I still had to watch out for her backhanded licks because they came without warning whenever she felt you deserved one of them. To be sure that Ma Jennie had gotten over me throwing away her glass cups, I eased up behind her to massage her shoulders and neck as she watched her favorite TV shows, "*The Price is Right*," and "*All My Children*". Afterward, she wanted to take a ride in the convertible I was driving at the time. While I was parading her around East Stuart, her beautiful gray hair was blowing in the wind as people we passed by spoke saying, "Hhheyyy, Maaa JJJennnie." She was having so much fun enjoying herself that she told me to stop by her friend Mrs. Magdalene's place (*a bar*) so that she could get in on the fun. It tickled Mrs. Mag to see Ma Jennie riding around in a convertible with her hair blowing in the wind. When we stopped in front of her place Mama said, "Come on and get in Mag." Ms. Mag said, "I'm too old to be riding in a convertible girl." Mama opened the door and said, "Child, get on in this car." With that invitation, she couldn't resist and got in.

We rode around East Stuart with the blues of B.B. King booming in the sound system. We were waving at everybody, and they were waving back as though we were in a parade. One of the onlookers said, "Ma Jennie, you and Mag got it going on," and Mrs. Mag said, "I know, that's right."

When Mother's Day came around, I bought my mother a Blazer and a large color television. She just cried joyfully and said, "What am I going to do with my Caddie and a Blazer." I jokingly said, "I will take the Caddie," but she said quickly, "You aren't going to take my car."

My mother having two cars didn't sit too well with her youngest sister, Helen (*Tiny*). Tiny is my favorite and closest aunt. She came to me privately with tears in her eyes and with some familiar lyrics by the Godfather of Soul, James Brown saying, "That ain't right, Turk, you done bought Jennie Mae two vehicles and you haven't bought my mom (*Viola/Fred/my grandmother*) a needed car." I said, "Tiny, Fred has never did anything for me," and that hurt Tiny because she really started to shed more tears. Her dripping Muck tears touched and got to me so I gave in and said, "Okay, okay, I will buy Fred a car."

Tiny thought I was kidding her until a week later I bought Fred her own Cadillac. That day I became the best nephew and the greatest grandson in the whole world. As far as I was concerned, every day was Mother's Day for Ma Jennie, which is why I provided her with everything I thought she wanted or needed.

On July 21, 1990 my second son, Adam George Jolly, was born a healthy baby boy. I held him in my arms proudly as one of the nurses took our picture. The little fella really brought a humbling sense of pride to my life.

One afternoon I went to get Candee and Adam to take them home. Their grandmother was very upset with me for putting her daughter through a drama-filled life. She had anticipated this particular moment patiently, to tell me what was on her mind while the kids were the only witnesses to the conversation. Before she gave me the kids' nourishment (*food bag she held in her hand*), she said in her Nassau (*Bahamian*) accent, "Turk, you know that you aren't any good. Why are you taking my daughter through so much hell? You just keep it up with your mess, I have a sister that will make you walk on water." I said, "Mrs. Mary, I have never walked on no water." If looks could kill, my funeral would have been the following week because the look she gave me, it was nothing nice.

Then my chauffeur, Eric Langston, walked in and she said to him, "Why are you hanging out with this hoodlum? Turk is no good and you shouldn't be hanging out with him because you look like a very nice young man." Homegirl was a real piece of work who said what she meant and meant what she said. With the kids in my arms, I told Eric to get the bag from Mrs. Mary, "Since you are a very nice young man."

On my monthly visit to see my mother in Belle Glade, I walked in on a heated conversation between my mom and her boyfriend, Sweetback Willie Dee. When I didn't

get my normal greeting kiss and hug from my mom,
I knew from the look on her face it was something serious.
Knowing that my mother had been in a previous abusive
relationship after she separated from my father, I had a
few serious words for Sweet Dee before I left concerning my old G (*girl*). I cut straight to the point with him,
not even playing with it—"That's Mama!" I don't play
about Mama.

Sweet Dee tried to explain their situation to me but
doing so only upset my mother even more. So, I said,
"Look man, you and I are cool but I'm not getting between
you and my mom. Just do both of us a favor, PLEASE do
not put your hands on my mother! Please, Sweet Dee,
I really mean that." On that note, I gave my mom a hug
and a kiss and cleared it. Willie Dee adhered to my warning because I didn't get any SOS signs from my mother.

On the weekend of September 9, 1990, two days before my
26th birthday, I took my parents, Cool Breeze and Jennie
Mae out on the town in Belle Glade. We had a great time
together with laughs and drinks as we took photos. Jennie
Mae and I even danced together. It turned out to be a
memorable moment for us because it was our last time
together.

Eighteen

God Will Take Care of Them

ON MAY 3, 1991, my third daughter, Raven Jolly was born. Two months later my youngest daughter, Turquoise Michelle Jolly (Q), was born on July 15, 1991. That same week, I accepted a call from Mike in prison during which he expressed the need to see me.

It was a ten-hour drive to visit Mike in North Florida at Okaloosa C.I. Steve and I stopped over in Tallahassee to catch Bell Biv Devoe and Johnny Gill live in concert. After the concert, we hung out at the Moon nightclub before visiting Mike the next morning.

Back home after visiting Mike, I stopped by his parents' house to make sure things were good with them. His mother, Mrs. Atline, was the only one home and boy did she have some words for me concerning the way I was living. She was a no-nonsense usher and mother in the Macedonia church I attended. She always addressed me by my childhood name whenever she talked to me. Mrs.

Atline asked, "Turkey Red, when are you going to stop selling that poison and get your life together with the Lord?" The only answer I had for her was, "Mrs. Atline, just pray for me." When I got ready to leave, she said "I am not through with you," but I insisted on leaving.

Apparently, she saw something spiritual coming my way. Right before I walked out of the door, she said "Turkey Red, what if something bad happens to you in them streets; what's going to happen to all of your children? Who is going to take care of them?" Without a thought or a blink of my eyes, I stated boldly "God will take care of them," and I was out the door.

One of my fun pastimes was attending Miami Dolphins home games with my posse. After the night games we were off to Club Rolex. What happens in the Lex stays in the Lex.

The roller coaster ride continued in my life. On the morning of October 5, 1991, I received news that my youngest son was born. That news was a real shocker because I only had sex with his mother once in February. As it turned out Leryia proved to be my third son.

In the month of November, my chauffeur, Eric, put me into the mix with his cousin in the Dirty South in Miami. He claimed his people knew some people in the underground world who "had it like that," so I gave it a test run. On our way to the Dirty South, I stopped to shop at the 79th Street Flea Market in Miami. To my surprise, a hundred and twenty miles from home, I ran into my three-year-old daughter, Candee, Mrs. Scott, and a few other females who were all in her daughter's upcoming wedding. I tried to avoid being seen by Candee, but it was too late because the moment she spotted me she flipped out and started screaming, "My daddy, my daddy, my daddy!" I tried to leave her with them but she cried all the more, so Mrs. Scott decided that it was best for Candee to go with me because she was determined to be with her daddy.

Meeting Eric's cousin at his father's house in Miami, everything seemed cool. Twenty minutes after I put five stacks (*one thousand dollars per stack*) in Eric's cousin's hand, he came back empty handed with a lame story. It was then I realized that I was robbed strong armed without a gun. Immediately, my first thought was to kill Eric and his cousin and then burn his father's house down to the ground. The only person who really stopped me from transforming into Jason (*character from Friday the 13th horror movie*) was my precious daughter Candee. I knew something could go wrong potentially and I didn't want to put her life in harm's way, so fortunately for Eric and his cousin, they were granted a stay of execution.

In my next move, I had Eric drive me to his cousin's mother's house in Miami. I knew that every mother loves her child and would do almost anything to keep them out of trouble. I figured that she would tell her son to give me back my money after I threatened to harm him. When Eric knocked on the door his cousin's mother opened it and to my surprise there were several young people singing a church song in the living room. She was surprised to see Eric in Miami and I was even more surprised when she invited us warmly to join in on the Bible study. This had to be an act of God because I sure didn't come to Miami to attend a Bible study.

She wanted to talk about Jesus, and I wanted to talk about my five stacks. All of a sudden, my position and intention weakened quickly because I knew that I was in the presence of someone who truly loved and served the Lord. As nicely as I knew how, I told her that her son took my money and I wanted it back. Her response was polite, kind and to the point. She said, "Baby, I have put my son's life in the hands of the Lord; I don't get involved with his street life." Then she said, "The only thing I could do for you and my son is pray for you two." Before I could respond she went right into prayer asking God for His intervention and blessings in Jesus' name. With that prayer, it was over because it humbled me enough to accept that loss and charge it to the game as we headed back home to Martin County.

On December 7, 1991, after setting it off in a hyped party at the Cadillac Nightclub in Indiantown, my life crashed into near fatality. Coming home at 3:30 a.m., Jay-1, Devine Clemons, and I were in a head-on collision with all of my music equipment in the back of my pickup truck. Just before the wreck, I begged Jay-1 to pull over as the oncoming car was swerving toward us at a very high rate of speed. Seconds before the impact, the last words I heard were Jay-1 telling me, "I got this Dirty. You don't even have a fishing license . . ." BOOM! The next thing I knew, I was waking up in Martin Memorial Hospital with a bloody face and a serious back injury. After Woodrow Jackson busted into the hospital pasting security to see if I was still alive, they shot me up with their legal drugs and released me once the police made known who I really was. It took me two weeks to recover physically before I got back into the groove of things.

With Christmas approaching, I had to deal with some Mama drama demands concerning one of my shorties. I didn't need a reminder of my responsibilities toward my children because Ma Jennie had prophesied to me at the age of eleven that I had better take care of every one of them.

The pressure of my life was flowing very fast in several directions. My people, in the know, who had inside information tipped me off to the latest scoop. A big round up was going down real soon and I was definitely in the mix of it. So, I decided to meet the financial needs and wants of all my children. I didn't realize that more than anything, they just wanted and needed me to be there for them as their father. I bought a needed Astro Van for the family.

For fun early Sunday mornings, I would ride the neighborhood winos in the van around East Stuart with the side door open. I played their favorite blues and oldies as they drank the liquor I bought for them. It was always fun and resulted in great laughter.

My parents, Wenzel and Jennie Jolly

Great Grandparents, Henry & Jennie Griffin

Grandmother Viola Glover

My mother, Jennie Mae Jolly

My parents, Wenzel (Cool Breeze), Jennie Mae Jolly

Brother Arthur Glover (winehead), brother Lincoln Jolly (Duck), me, and mom

Adam Jolly, Aunt Helen, Uncle Jerry O Bryant (O.B), Uncle Jimmy Glover (Ski-Bo), Aunt Alfreda, Uncle Ralph Glover (Bean), Uncle Irvin Griffin (Nappie Chin), brother Lincoln Jolly (Duck), cousin Shawn (Muck) and Grandmother Viola Glover's (Fred) 93rd Birthday party

Helen, Jimmy, me, Roxann, Alfreda, Irvin, and Grandma Viola

Visiting Mickie in prison. (l to r) Adam, Great Grandmother Jennie Griffin, and Uncle Charles Glover (Mickie)

My brother, Lincoln Jolly (Duck) cousin Mr Cooper, and me

Adam Jolly DJing in the club

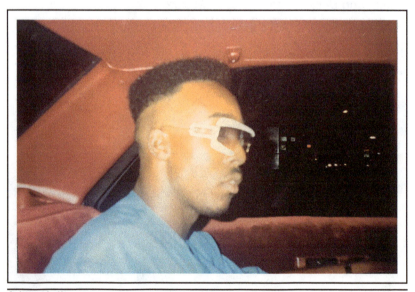

Adam Jolly

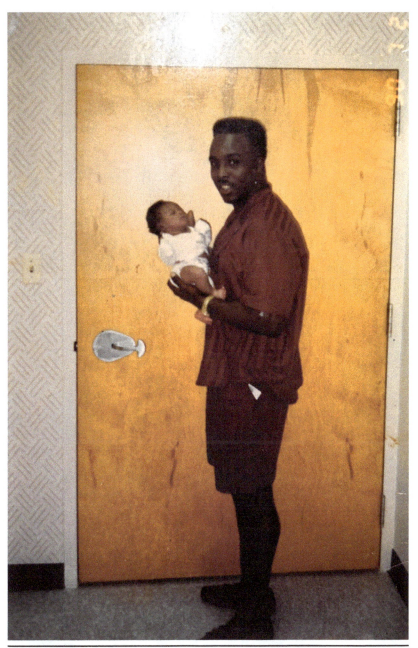

My son Adam and me

Me, Mom Jennie Mae, and Uncle Jimmy Glover (Ski-Bo)

Adam holding daughter Candee

Adam in Port of Miami

Close-up of Adam Jolly

Adam at Hard Rock Cafe

Adam Jolly-1988

My daughter Candee, grandson Marcus and son Lyria in a prison visitation

My daughter's Candee, Raven, Marcus and me

My son, Adam, me, and daughter, Candee

Daughter Turquoise & grandson Jayden, daughter Candee & grandson Marcus, and me

Receiving my Doctorate Degree (2021)

Nineteen

They Thought Evil Against Me, but God . . .

THOUGH I WAS the bad guy on the police radar and by certain peoples' standards, I helped a lot of unfortunate families and friends with their finances willfully during their times of desperate need. I donated my time, music, and jet skis to help out with the disabled children along with Mr. Jay Thompson and Mrs. Linda Smith, who were community activists and historians. I also assisted Mr. Thompson with the annual Black History programs and helped the troubled kids at the Spectrum Alternative School.

Even though I was a sinner I still tithed at Macedonia and gave decent offerings to other churches. In my heart I believed I was paying God off. I even wore a big gold cross on a nice Gucci gold chain around my neck. None of my good deeds, tithes, or offerings that I gave could stop the inevitable from going down in my life.

On January 31, 1992, I was arrested for selling crack cocaine along with twenty-one other men in an undercover operation. While I was in the Martin County Jail Ma Jennie had been diagnosed with Alzheimer's disease as her mind and memory began to deteriorate.

Thirteen months later, on February 23, 1993, I was found guilty. The very moment the jury foreperson announced the word "guilty", I heard God's quiet voice in my heart clearly for the first time saying, You can't put any man or anyone else before me." The verdict crushed my family and friends as they sat in disbelief in the audience. Bean and Wine Head were already doing time in prison. Bean received 22 years for attempted murder for shooting another man who played with his money. Wine Head, who was only supposed to receive 22 years, received 50 years for selling drugs and for popping off (*cussing*) at Judge Schack before he was sentenced.

On April 23, 1993, I was sentenced to 50 years as a habitual offender (H.O.) with a mandatory 15 years to be served in the DOC. Living a thug life had finally caught up with me, causing me to lose my freedom at a great cost. What really pained me the most was the fact that I was leaving my kids without their father to help raise them.

I arrived at Madison C.I. in May 1993 with the same unacceptable criminal behavior. I grew weary as I continued to hustle and flow in the game. I started to feel disgusted with the predicament I had put myself in.

On July 5, 1994, my hero and soul inspiration, Mrs. Jennie Griffin, passed away gracefully in her full golden age. Ma Jennie was full of compassion and life. She impacted countless peoples' lives. She was stronger within than a man, sharp on her feet, prompt in affairs, and she enjoyed and celebrated life. She was loved by everybody and made wise decisions like a commanding chief, with unconditional love. Ma Jennie will live forever in the hearts of her descendants and friends.

Not long after Ma Jennie passed, I started to attend church services during which I sensed, for the first time, an urgency to be saved.

Meanwhile, my cousin Mike had gotten saved in prison. After he got out, he stopped by to visit me in Madison. His conversation was Christ-centered, which was strange coming from him, but I still heard him out on what he had to say about salvation. Since Mike was running a little late for a pastoral conference in Jacksonville with Bishop T.D. Jakes, he had to go. Before he left, he prayed for me to have my own personal experience with Jesus Christ.

Shortly thereafter a certain Christian inmate started witnessing to me about Jesus every time he saw me. I tried to intimidate him with a prison tactic, but he looked me right into my eyes and said boldly, "What's in me is greater and more powerful than what is in you."

I didn't understand his words, but I sensed a force behind what he said. I couldn't shake this Christian off my trail, so I agreed to listen to a preacher on the radio named Tony Evans. He not only made sense when teaching the Word of God, but he sounded just like Richard Pryor. After we listened to Tony Evans this Christian inmate shared two things with me that I will never forget. First, he said, " You are in the wrong army." Second, "When you surrender your life to Jesus you are going to be a force to be reckoned with because you are going to be a five-star general in God's Kingdom."

One day I attended a Chapel service during which Evangelist Betty Jenkins preached a word from the Bible that spoke to my heart. However, when she gave an altar call, I hardened my heart and didn't respond.

During the first week of November 1996, an inmate had to be airlifted out of Madison due to a serious head injury. Because I had the lock on most of the flow at Madison, it was the haters' perfect scenario for getting me off the compound. An anonymous source dropped a dime on me which was far from the truth. The anonymous lie fingered me as the perpetrator and got me removed from the open compound. I was placed in Administrative Confinement (A/C) pending investigation, along with several other inmates who were associated with me. My stuttering classification officer, Mr. Muse, came to see me in A/C to tell me that he didn't know I was rolling like that and that the administration was out to nail me. As I entertained my limited options, I concluded that my back was against the wall and I had no way out of this jam.

After the normal procedural count time (*roll call*) a fishing line was thrown perfectly under my locked cell door from the hold down man (*he was holding drugs for me*) in another locked down cell. At the end of the fishing line was a lit stick of Mary J. Once I was under the influence of Mary J, I found myself cutting a deal with God by telling Him that if He get me out of this jam I would serve Him with all my heart. Not realizing who I was really talking to or what I was saying, I told God that I wasn't ready to surrender my life to Him. Then I asked God if He would give me a little more time to handle my business. I would throw my hands in with the game and hustling and come clean with Him.

The very next thing I knew I was on my knees telling God how disgusted I was with my life and that I was sorry for the way I was living. I opened the Bible while I was still on my knees and began to read a verse I had never seen or heard before: "If you confess with your mouth the Lord Jesus and believe in your heart that God has raised Him from the dead, you will be saved" (*Romans 10:9*). Immediately after reading, believing, and confessing this scripture, something happened inside me. As I stood up I felt that the weight of my burdens had lifted and the feeling of guilt and shame were gone.

As the high of Mary J evaporated, I felt a real sense of peace and joy had been released into the empty void of my soul. The reality was that I had just genuinely accepted Jesus Christ into my heart to be my personal Lord and Savior based upon the authority of God's Word in 2 Peter 3:9, "The Lord is not slack concerning His promise, as some count slackness, but is longsuffering toward us, not willing that any should perish but that all should come to repentance," and Romans 10:9 (*quoted above*). This life-changing experience took place on Sunday night, November 17, 1996. From that day forward I never had the desire to smoke Mary J, or the desire to hustle or sell drugs any more. At that time, with a clean heart and a right mind, I told God whatever His will was for my life, I would do it.

The first people I told that I was saved were the guys who were down with me in crime. They thought I was losing my mind because they started saying that my time was bugging me up and this was a plot to get out of jail. When they asked me what was going on and what I meant when I said I was saved, I explained to them what had happened to me, but they still didn't believe me.

I sent the word out to my homeboys on the compound to let them know I was saved. I told Rodney Hamilton (*Creeper*) and Henry Harris (*TY*) (*like me, they both were from Martin County*) they could split the product, the money, and the canteen (*illegal operation*) that I left them to oversee. I also sent word to all my debtors to let them know they no longer owed me because I was out of the game. My mind was made up as I was fully persuaded that I wasn't going to be like the Godfather, Al Pacino, and allow them to pull me back into the game.

When I stopped the Mary J and my business operations from flowing, my boyz in confinement knew that I was serious about being saved. It became obvious to me that my strongest critics and all my haters thought evil against me, but God meant it for good because He had a plan and purpose for my life.

Then one day a saved Correctional Sergeant, who I used to give a hard time to, came to my cell door. He said, "Come here." When I stood at the door, he said, "The word on the compound is that you are saved. Is that right?"

I said, "Yes sir, that's right."

Then he said, "How do you know that you are really saved?"

I picked up my Bible to read 2 Peter 3:9 and Romans 10:9 – 13 and responded, "Based upon the authority of God's Word I am saved and have a right relationship with God through Jesus Christ."

He said, "Man, you are serious. I want you to know that I am proud of you. I know that you are going to make a difference in the Kingdom leading lost people to Jesus."

Before he left, he prayed with me to be encouraged, keep the faith, and always look to Jesus. Then Mr. Muse, my classification officer, came by to tell me that the administration had decided to transfer me further west on I-10 to Century C.I., Pensacola, Florida. I pleaded with him to put me in to be transferred to Cross City C.I.

On January 17, 1997 I arrived at Cross City, which is where I was raised up in the Word of God. On my first day there, during the reception process, a White female sergeant called me into a room where she was sitting alone behind a desk. As soon as I walked in by myself, she started popping off loudly and repeatedly saying, "Why are you disrespecting me like that?" I just stood there in front of the desk looking at her like she was crazy.

I didn't see it coming, what was about to happen. After about twenty seconds of her failed antics of trying to get me to blow, five White sergeants rushed into the room to threaten me further with their D.O.C. intimidation tactics. One of them got to within a few inches of my face and was cussing me out loudly as a few drops of his saliva hit my face. He said, "Why did you disrespect this female officer, boy?"

In my heart I was already praying, asking God why He was allowing these Klansmen to do me like this. You know, I had just accepted Jesus two months ago and I have to go through this confrontation.

From my Lake Butler D.O.C. experience and the convict code, I knew it was wise for me to not respond to the deceptive questions of these "good ole redneck boys". That is, I knew that whatever I said, they were going to twist my words against me to potentially jump on me or hit me and then it would have really been on.

Standing with my hands positioned freely behind my back, I remained silent in response to their intense questioning. When they finally concluded that I wasn't falling for the bait to entrap me, their strategy changed. Finally, one of them said, "We know all about you and your hustling game you had going on at Madison. We received a call from Madison concerning how you operated over there. We aren't having any of that here at Cross City. The first time we hear of any illegal activity or drug movement associated with Adam Jolly, we will deal with you and have you on the first ride smoking out of Cross City."

Then the female sergeant informed me, sarcastically, that I would be assigned to work on the gun squad. They thought evil against me, but God's divine plan and purpose for my life was being set in motion.

My homeboy Calvin Jackson (*Reb*) was there at Cross City. When he saw me the first thing he said was "Boy, it's on now." Reb, who knew me since I was a shorty (*young child*), used to regulate the product for me on the streets. In fact, Reb was one of the men who was arrested with me in the undercover drug operation named "Custer," on January 31, 1992, in Stuart. The State made an example out of Reb by giving him a life sentence for two dime (*ten dollar*) cocaine rocks. When I told Reb that I was saved, he said Yeah right man, your name is ranging throughout the D.O.C. Who do you think you are fooling? I know you personally Turkey Red. It's just a matter of time. Just put it in my hand whenever you decide to make it happen and you know I got it."

My daily walk with the Lord proved to Reb that I was as serious as anthrax about being saved and serving the Lord. For my personal spiritual growth and development, I attended faithfully the weekly Chapel Christian services and Bible studies the Body of Christ conducted out on the recreation field under the leadership of Ernest Atterbury. I was encouraged to know that it took genuine fellowship with the brethren to help strengthen my spiritual growth and to have someone with whom I could be held accountable. More importantly, I couldn't neglect the Word of God and expect to become a mature Christian.

Early in my Christian walk, I struggled spiritually because I didn't understand clearly that it was a faith walk. In the Bible study I was taught that faith (*confidence, assurance, believing, and trust*) comes by hearing and hearing by the Word of God. [*Romans 10:17*[1]; *2 Corinthians 5:7*[2]] I had a rocky start in my Christian walk, with self-control, profanity, and drinking buck (*prison brewed wine*). I ignorantly justified my actions.

I learned in a Rock of Ages prison ministry seminar that I have a soul and a spirit according to the Word of God. [*1 Thessalonians 5:23*[3]; *Hebrews 4:12*[4]] Our souls consist of our mind, will, and emotions. Our minds are where we imagine things and think our thoughts — it's our intellect. [*Proverbs 23:7*[5]] Our will gives us the ability to choose and make decisions. [*Matthew 16:24 – 25*[6]; *Deuteronomy 30:19*[7]; *Joshua 24:15*[8]] Our emotions give us the ability to translate our feelings. [*Mark 12:30*[9]] This is why our mind, will, and emotions are considered to be at the very seat of our souls. Because the Word says, "I am a new creature in Christ," I had to discipline myself to renew my mind with the Word of God. [*2 Corinthians 5:17*[10]; *Ephesians 4:23*[11]; *Romans 12:12*[12]; *2 Timothy 2:15*[13]]

It was revealed to me that the real me is the regenerated spirit that is my inward, inner and hidden man, who needs to be renewed and strengthened with the Word of God. [*2 Corinthians 4:16*[14]; *Ephesians 3:16*[15]; *1 Peter 3:4*[16]] It's a gradual process called sanctification (*to set apart, to separate, to position you for God's service*) [*2 Thessalonians 2:13*[17]; *John 17:7*[18]; *2 Corinthians 6:17*[19]] To establish a structured and balanced Christian life, I began to pray consistently and daily, and to fast as the Holy Spirit prompted (*led me to do*). [*Matthew 6:5 – 6*[20], *16 – 18*[21]]

Meanwhile, I went to work for three months in thirty-degree weather on the gun squad (*group of inmates digging ditches under supervision of armed corrections officers*). We worked outside the institution around a nearby airport from 6:00 a.m. to 3:00 p.m. Monday through Friday. I had to work with iron leg shackles around my ankles alongside thirty-six other inmates. This work assignment was designed for rebellious inmates with the intent of punishing and disciplining them the hard way for having received Disciplinary Reports (DRs). We worked with bush axes and shovels to cut down and root up tree stumps and dug ditches only to cover them up when done. Four officers watched us closely while they carried shotguns and automatic handguns. Two major rules were stipulated that had to be obeyed while working on the gun squad: First, whenever we heard an officer's whistle blow, it was mandatory that we fall face down immediately, right where we were standing. Falling on the ground was for each inmate's benefit. That is, in the event an inmate on the work squad tried to escape, the inmates who were face down on the ground wouldn't get shot while the officers tried to shoot the inmate who was attempting to escape, and second, no talking was tolerated unless it was in response to an officer's question. No inmate was allowed to talk at any time while working. We were only allowed to talk during our twenty-minute lunch break. Talking resulted in unwanted consequences with a longer stay on the gun squad.

That female sergeant and her clique thought evil against me, but God meant it for my good because His plan was serving His Kingdom's purpose in my life. Knowing that I couldn't talk for eight hours I started packing my pocket-sized Bible so I could quote scripture to myself and meditate on God's Word throughout the day. This is how I learned to remember the Word of God by heart. My relationship with the Lord began to become a reality to me as Jesus revealed Himself in my spirit by the Word of God. [*John 14:16*[22], *21*[23]; *1 Samuel 3:21*[24]] When I read in the word that God said when I get saved, He will save my house, I sent all my children a pocket-sized Bible believing God for their salvation. [*Acts 16:30 – 31*[25]; *Isaiah 55:11*[26]; *Numbers 23:19*[27]]

My most difficult test on the gun squad came when I was placed in confinement because I complained that the iron chains were too tight around my ankles. The sergeant in charge thought evil against me, but God meant it for my good because He had a plan and purpose for allowing me to be locked up.

In confinement, God wanted me to identify with a character in the Bible named Joseph. Joseph was despised and rejected because of his God-given spiritual gift and favor that was on his life. Joseph's own brothers meant evil when they put him in a pit without water, leaving him for dead, but God meant it for Joseph's good.

Though Joseph had a relationship with the Lord, he still was accused of rape and was falsely imprisoned. Yet again, God meant it for Joseph's good. God blessed Joseph tremendously as he forgave his brothers, blessed his family, and helped save countless lives.

After three days of reading and learning about Joseph, God blessed me out of confinement with a Kingdom perspective, Genesis Chapters 37–50.

ENDNOTES

1 "So then faith comes by hearing, and hearing by the Word of God."
2 "For we walk by faith, not by sight."
3 "Now may the God of peace Himself sanctify you completely; and may your whole spirit, soul, and body be preserved blameless at the coming of our Lord Jesus Christ."
4 "For the word of God is living and powerful, and sharper than any two-edged sword, piercing even to the division of soul and spirit, and of joints and marrow, and is a discerner of the thoughts and intents of the heart."
5 "For as he thinks in his heart, so is he."
6 "Then Jesus said to His disciples, 'if anyone desires to come after Me, let him deny himself, take up his cross, and follow Me. For whoever desires to save his life will lose it, but whoever loses his life for my sake will find it.'"
7 "I call heaven and the earth as witnesses today against you, that I have set before you life and death, blessing and cursing; therefore, choose life, that both you and your descendants may live."
8 "And if it seems evil to you to serve the Lord, choose for yourselves this day whom you will serve, whether the gods which your fathers served that

were on the other side of the River, or the gods of the Amorites, in whose
land you dwell. But as for me and my house, we will serve the Lord."
9 "And you shall love the Lord your God with all your heart, with all
your soul, with all your mind, and with all your strength. This is the first
commandment."
10 "Therefore, if anyone is in Christ, he is a new creation; old things have
passed away; behold, all things have become new."
11 "And be renewed in the spirit of your mind."
12 "And do not be conformed to this world, but be transformed by the
renewing of your mind, that you may prove what is that good and acceptable
and perfect will of God."
13 "Be diligent to present yourself approved to God, a worker who does
not need to be ashamed, rightly dividing the word of truth."
14 "Therefore, we do not lose heart. Even though our outward man is perishing, yet the inward man is being renewed day by day."
15 "That He would grant you, according to the riches of His glory, to be
strengthened with might through His spirit in the inner man."
16 "Rather let it be the hidden person of the heart, with the incorruptible
beauty of a gentle and quiet spirit, which is very precious in the sight of
God."
17 "But we are bound to give thanks to God always for you, brethren
beloved by the Lord, because God from the beginning chose you for salvation through sanctification by the Spirit and belief in the truth."
18 "Now they have known that all things which You have given Me are from
You."
19 "Therefore, 'Come out from among them And be separate, says the Lord.
Do not touch what is unclean, And I will receive you.'"
20 "And when you pray, you shall not be like the hypocrites. For they love
to pray standing in the synagogues and on the corners of the streets, that
they may be seen by men. Assuredly, I say to you, they have their reward. But
you, when you pray, go into your room, and when you have shut your door,
pray to your Father who is in the secret place; and your Father who sees in
secret will reward you openly."
21 "Moreover, when you fast, do not be like the hypocrites, with a sad
countenance. For they disfigure their faces that they may appear to men to
be fasting. Assuredly, I say to you, they have their reward. But you, when you
fast, anoint your head and wash your face, so that you do not appear to men
to be fasting, but to your Father who is in the secret place; and your Father
who sees in secret will reward you openly."
22 "And I will pray the Father, and He will give you another Helper, that He
may abide with you forever."
23 "He who has My commandments and keeps them, it is he who loves me.
And he who loves Me will be loved by my Father, and I will love him and

manifest Myself to him."

24 "Then the Lord appeared again in Shiloh. For the Lord revealed Himself to Samuel in Shiloh by the word of the Lord."

25 "And he brought them out and said, 'Sirs, what must I do to be saved?' So they said, 'Believe on the Lord Jesus Christ, and you will be saved, you and your household'"

26 "So shall My word be that goes forth from My mouth; it shall not return to Me void, But it shall accomplish what I please, and it shall prosper in the thing for which I sent it."

27 "God is not a man that He should lie, nor a son of man, that He should repent. Has He said, and He will not do? Or has He spoken, and will He not make it good?"

Twenty

Called and Anointed for the Kingdom

ON MARCH 24, 1997, I was baptized by Reverend Lorenzo Robinson at Faith Chapel. It was a special Kingdom moment that expressed outwardly my inward confession that I am saved, and that my mind is made up and that my heart is fixed on following Jesus. I received encouraging letters from Woodrow Jackson (*Woody*) who was at Martin C.I., which inspired me to take this leap of faith. In fact, Woody is Reb's brother, who got arrested with us on January 31, 1992. After sixty days in jail, Woody received Christ and has been a solid example of a devout Christian since that time.

On a rare day off from the gun squad, the Lord ordered my steps to the Chapel where I was the last believer to enroll in a six-month Evangelism Explosion (EE) class. Arthur (*Art*) Hallett is the president of the EE Prison Ministry under Dr. D. James Kennedy Ministries. For six months Art taught and trained me how to win lost souls for the Kingdom. I received my certification in EE as a teacher and trainer in the EE Ministry.

I learned real fast while witnessing to lost souls on the battlefield that no amount of class time or training supersedes the Word of God. One day, I witnessed to an unsaved inmate who had one question for me. Specifically, he asked "Aren't you that same drug dealer who was at Madison selling all those drugs and running a gambling operation?"

I felt like a deer caught in the headlights, but I had to give him an honest answer, so I said, Yes, I was that man. Continuing further with the only answer I could give him at the time, I said "I am not that man or drug dealer anymore."

"How is that when I am standing here looking at you and talking to you?"

"My Bible tells me that I am a new creature in Christ and if that's who God says I am, that's who I am in Him" (*2 Corinthians 5:17*[1]). I had made up my mind that I wasn't going to allow anyone or my incarceration to define who I am. I wasn't looking for anyone to validate me because I knew within myself that I was saved and truly serving the Lord. That encounter alone taught me that I really needed to become a student of the Word of God and build an altar in my heart for Jesus so that I would always be ready to give an answer for my faith in God. [*1 Peter 3:15*[2]]

Because of my heart's desire to see lost souls saved, the revelation of Galatians 5:16[3] and Romans 8:14[4] enlightened my spiritual understanding, enabling me to witness for Jesus effectively. Walking in and being led by the Spirit is following and living passionately in the counsel of God's Word. This is how believers know when to and when not to speak, as the Spirit leads them. Jesus said, "The words that I speak to you are spirit, and they are life" (*John 6:63,*[5] *68*[6]).

As Christians, we are to share the Word because we are communicators of eternal life for Jesus. After I prayed about it, I had my four gold tooth caps removed. The next time Reb saw me, he asked "Where are the gold teeth?" I said, "At the dentist's office." He got very upset with me because I wouldn't go get them for him to sell on the compound.

Excited about being saved, I to wrote my family and those who I thought would rejoice with me because I had given my life to the Lord. Boy was I wrong. Believe it or not, some were actually mad because I had given my life to God. In fact, when the flow stopped coming in, Fred (*my grandmother*) and Tiny visited me to see what was really going on with me. While Tiny and I talked, Fred sat quietly for about an hour staring me down with her big pop eyes before she said anything. The first thing Fred said came as a shocker to Tiny but not to me because I had learned not to put anything past her.

Fred looked me square in my face as I sat beside her and said boldly, "Negro, if you don't quit playing with God you are going to Hell." Immediately, I leaned closer to look in her pop eyes directly and said, "If you don't repent of your sins and receive Jesus, Negro, you are the one who is going to Hell."

As she grabbed my shirt with her left hand, she put me in a tight headlock with her right hand and arm. Meanwhile, Tiny was punching me and telling me not to talk to her mother like that. I said, "She was the one who started this."

Fred said, "I will still beat your butt in front of these White folks." After she interrogated me about how I got saved, I attempted to witness to her, but it was difficult for her to receive the Word of God from her grandson. As far as she was concerned, in her mind, I was still in the game of hustling, but I had cut her off because I wasn't sending her any more flow. Of all people, Fred the gangster tried to pull me back into the game.

When I called Jennie Mae (*my mother*) to tell her the good news that I had gotten saved, she was the first one to rejoice with me. She said, "Turk, baby, Mama is so happy for you."

I called my mom once a week. Mama told me not to call on Thursday nights. When I asked her why not, she said. "My fine men come on TV at 8:00 p.m."

I asked, "Mama, what men are you talking about?"

She responded, "The Rock and Stone Cold on Smackdown."

"Mama, please."

"Baby, The Rock is the finest thang on TV but Stone Cold Austin is the man."

The second person who rejoiced with me was Mrs. Matheny, my elderly friend. She was so thrilled and excited for me.

Meanwhile at Cross City I disciplined myself to spend quality time in my Bible and took my devotional time with the Lord more seriously. The Word of God began to transform my character from the inside out and empowered me to do God's will. This is why God gave me a new heart and a new spirit to do His will. [*Ezekiel 36:26–27*[7]; *Philippians 2:13*[8]]

During October 1997 I received the baptism of the Holy Ghost for God's service and to advance His Kingdom. Receiving the gift of the Holy Spirit was evident when I began to walk in power and authority. [*Acts 2:38*[9]; *Acts 1:8*[10]] The same night I experienced a demonic attack from an assigned demon. I literally saw a demon attempting to devour me. As soon as I rebuked him in Jesus' name, I watched him disintegrate into a thousand pieces. After I experienced and saw that, I said It's on now—I got it." The Devil was putting up a fight for my allegiance which had been reconciled back to God. That is, I had defected to God's army from my position as a front-line general in the Devil's army. God had placed a burning fire inside me that the fire departments can't put out. Spiritually, I now felt like Muhammad Ali sporting a knock-out punch in my arsenal.

BREAKING NEWS—the Devil is a bad paymaster. I know because I served him faithfully for thirty-two years and he hasn't paid me yet. I'm on the Lord's side now and I'm good.

It was at Cross City where God called and anointed me for his Kingdom to teach and preach the Gospel of Christ. I began to renew my mind in the Word with a compelling urgency and received deliverance from strongholds in my soul that were hindering my relationship with God. Then, I discovered my gift and my calling in the faith, which is to operate in the office of an Evangelist. My character and walk were consistent with the calling upon my life and the Word of God was confirming in my spirit the messages I preached. I yielded my life willfully and obediently, identifying with Jesus Christ and Phillip the Evangelist, to make my calling and election sure. [*Matthew 10:13*[11], *7–8*[12]; *Acts 8:5–8*[13], *26–40*[14], *21:8*[15]; *2 Peter 1:10*[16]]

It was my first time ministering the Word of God under the anointing unto the body of Christ and to the lost souls out on the recreation field. I understood in my calling that evangelism and discipleship are not the same, but they are both critical in leading others to Jesus and building them up in the Word to follow Jesus. In other words, evangelism is sharing and explaining the Gospel (*the goodness of Jesus' death, burial, and resurrection [1 Corinthians 15:3–4*[17]]) to lead the lost to Christ after they repent.

Once a sinner accepts Jesus Christ, only then are they in position to be a disciple in the Word to follow Jesus. Discipleship means to teach believers in the faith to learn and follow after Jesus' teaching in the Word of God. This is why it is impossible to disciple a sinner when they haven't repented and received Jesus Christ.

When I got off the gun squad, I told God He didn't have to put me in a wheelchair for me to serve Him. I began to plead the blood of Jesus over all my children in my prayers and that God would bless their going out and coming in, Exodus 12:15,[18] Proverbs 20:7,[19] and Isaiah 44:3.[20]

One of the prison volunteers who had come to minister, Reverend Lorenzo Robinson, said that God told him to bless me with a Hebrew-Greek study Bible. Upon receiving that Bible, I became more acquainted with Jesus in His Word and in my prayer life. I also noticed that my desire for Him increased. The revelation of God's Word began to deliver me from myself as ungodly habits started to drop off of me. My discernment of sin sharpened as the indwelling Holy Spirit convicted me of what was right and wrong as he grew louder in my conscience. False teaching and wrong thinking became more obvious as I accumulated more truth within my spirit. The Holy Spirit began to enable me to care for people who previously were either unnoticed or difficult to get along with. I not only began to know the Word and began quoting scripture, I also began to know the God of the Word by His power.

Being called and anointed for the Kingdom, I didn't know that I had to count the costs associated with my endeavors to help advance God's Kingdom. I began to understand that God called me out of the darkness of sin with His purpose to follow Jesus. Becoming a fisher of men. [*1 Peter 2:9*[21]; *2 Timothy 1:9*[22]; *Matthew 4:18–22*[23]] There is a price to pay to walk in God's anointing. Being anointed means to be consecrated (*devoted and dedicated*) for the Lord's service. Being anointed also speaks to God's presence and yoke-destroying power upon your life. It's the anointing that destroys yokes and removes heavy burdens. [*Isaiah 10:27*[24]] When God called and anointed me for His service, He released His supernatural empowerment upon me. [*Luke 4:18*[25]*; Acts 10:30*[26]*; Acts 1:8*[27]] Being anointed will bring opposition, persecution, rejection, envy, jealousy, and hatred. [*Genesis 37:5*[28]*; Psalm 2:1–3*[29]*; Psalm 105:14–15*[30]*; 2 Timothy 3:12*[31]]

Leading the first lost soul to Christ was a thrill and joy that I can't put into words. I just rejoiced with the young man and with the angels in Heaven upon his repentance and acceptance of Jesus based upon the authority of God's Word. [*Luke 15:10*[32]*; Romans 10:9–13*[33]] Witnessing and ministering the Word of God led to several confrontations with those who opposed the Gospel of Jesus. Standing for God, I have witnessed countless times when God stood for me by honoring His Word in my life. [*Exodus 14:13–14,*[34] *23:22*[35]*; Deuteronomy 28:7*[36]*; Psalm 46:1*[37]*; Proverbs 16:7*[38]]

To establish balance in my Christian walk, during my free time when I was not reading or studying my Bible, I worked out with weights and played sports. Daily, I listened to Gospel music and preaching on the radio. At certain times of the day, I would also listen to sports to keep up with my Yankees, Sixers, Raiders, and Seminoles. These habits have persisted to this day.

I wrote to all my children often and never missed their birthdays by sending them cards to encourage their hearts. Every Mother's Day I would send my children's mothers Mother's Day cards that expressed my appreciation for taking care of my responsibilities during my absence. In fact, I took the initiative to bring closure to a dark chapter in my life concerning all the promiscuous relationships I had. After praying for God's wisdom and the appropriate words, I wrote each of those women asking for their forgiveness for the hurt and pain I had caused. Though they each had moved on with their lives, I cleared my conscience before God and got the residual of any lingering feelings and thoughts of infatuation off of my spirit.

ENDNOTES

1 "Therefore, if anyone is in Christ, he is a new creation; old things have passed away; behold, all things have become new."
2 "But sanctify the Lord God in your hearts, and always be ready to give a defense to everyone who asks you a reason for the hope that is in you, with meekness and fear."
3 "I say then: Walk in the Spirit, and you shall not fulfill the lust of the flesh."
4 "For as many as are led by the Spirit of God, these are sons of God."
5 "It is the Spirit who gives life; the flesh profits nothing. The words that I speak to you are spirit, and they are life."
6 "But Simon Peter answered Him, 'Lord, to whom shall we go? You have the words of eternal life."
7 "I will give you a new heart and put a new spirit within you; I will take the heart of stone out of your flesh and give you a heart of flesh."
8 "for it is God who works in you both to will and to do for His good pleasure."
9 "Then Peter said to them, 'Repent, and let every one of you be baptized in the name of Jesus Christ for the remission of sins; and you shall receive the gift of the Holy Spirit.'"
10 "But you shall receive power when the Holy Spirit has come upon you; and you shall be witnesses to Me in Jerusalem, and in all Judea and Samaria, and to the end of the earth."
11 "And when He had called His twelve disciples to Him, He gave them power over unclean spirits, to cast them out, and to heal all kinds of sickness and all kinds of disease. Now the names of the twelve apostles are these: first, Simon, who is called Peter, and Andrew his brother; James, the son of Zebedee, and John his brother; Philip and Bartholomew; Thomas and Matthew the tax collector; James the son of Alphaeus, and Labbaeus, whose surname was Thaddaeus."
12 "As you go, preach, saying, 'The Kingdom of Heaven is at hand.' Heal the sick, cleanse the lepers, raise the dead, cast out demons. Freely you have received, freely give."

13 "Then Philip went down to the city of Samaria and preached Christ to them. And the multitudes with one accord heeded the things spoken by Philip, hearing and seeing the miracles which he did. For unclean spirits, crying with a loud voice, came out of many who were possessed; and many who were paralyzed and lame were healed. And there was great joy in that city."

14 Philip preached to an Ethiopian Eunuch who, as a result, becomes a believer and is water baptized (*full immersion*) by Philip.

15 "On the next day we who were Paul's companions departed and came to Caesarea, and entered the house of Philip the evangelist, who was one of the seven, and stayed with him."

16 "Therefore, brethren, be even more diligent to make your call and election sure, for if you do these things you will never stumble."

17 "For I delivered to you first of all that which I also received: that Christ died for our sins according to the Scriptures, and that He was buried, and that He rose again the third day according to the Scriptures."

18 "Seven days you shall eat unleavened bread. On the first day you shall remove leaven from your houses. For whoever eats unleavened bread from the first day until the seventh day, that person shall be cut off from Israel."

19 "The righteous man walks in his integrity; His children are blessed after him."

20 "For I will pour water on him who is thirsty, and floods on the dry ground; I will pour My Spirit on your descendants, and My blessing on your offspring."

21 "But you are a chosen generation, a royal priesthood, a holy nation, His own special people, that you may proclaim the praises of Him who called you out of darkness into His marvelous light."

22 "Who has saved us and called us with a holy calling, not according to our works, but according to His own purpose and grace which was given to us in Christ Jesus before time began."

23 "But Jesus, walking by the Sea of Galilee, saw two brothers, Simon called Peter, and Andrew his brother, casting a net into the sea; for they were fishermen. Then He said to them, 'Follow me, and I will make you fishers of men.' They immediately left their nets and followed Him. Going on from there, He saw two other brothers, James the son of Zebedee, and John his brother, in the boat with Zebedee their father, mending their nets. He called them, and immediately they left their boat and their father, and followed Him."

24 "It shall come to pass in that day That his burden will be taken away from your shoulder, and his yoke from your neck, and the yoke will be destroyed because of the anointing oil."

25 "The Spirit of the Lord is upon me, Because He has anointed me To preach the Gospel to the poor; He has sent me to heal the brokenhearted,

To proclaim liberty to the captives And recovery of sight to the blind, To set at liberty those who are oppressed."

26 "So Cornelius said, four days ago I was fasting until this hour; and at the ninth hour I prayed in my house, and behold, a man stood before me in bright clothing."

27 "But you shall receive power when the Holy Spirit has come upon you; and you shall be witnesses to Me in Jerusalem, and in all Judea and Samaria, and to the end of the earth."

28 "Now Joseph had a dream, and he told it to his brothers; and they hated him even more."

29 "Why do the nations rage, A the people plot a vain thing? The kings of the earth set themselves, And the rulers take counsel together, Against the Lord and against His anointed, saying, 'Let us break Their bonds in pieces And cast away Their cords from us."

30 "He permitted no one to do them wrong; Yes, He rebuked kings for their sakes, Saying, 'Do not touch My anointed ones, And do My prophets no wrong.'"

31 "Yes, and all who desire to live Godly in Christ Jesus will suffer persecution."

32 "Likewise, I say to you, there is joy in the presence of the angels of God over one sinner who repents."

33 "if you confess with your mouth the Lord Jesus and believe in your heart that God has raised Him from the dead, you will be saved. For with the heart one believes unto righteousness, and with the mouth confession is made unto salvation. For the Scripture says, 'Whoever believes on Him will not be put to shame.' For there is no distinction between Jew and Greek, for the same Lord over all is rich to all who call upon Him. For 'whoever calls upon the name of the Lord shall be saved.'"

34 "And Moses said to the people, 'Do not be afraid. Stand still, and see the salvation of the Lord, which He will accomplish for you today. For the Egyptians whom you see today, you shall see again no more forever. The Lord will fight for you, and you shall hold your peace.'"

35 "But if you indeed obey His voice and do all that I speak, then I will be an enemy to your enemies and an adversary to your adversaries."

36 "The Lord will cause your enemies who rise against you to be defeated before your face; they shall come out against you one way and flee before you seven ways."

37 "God is our refuge and strength, A very present help in trouble."

38 "When a man's ways please the Lord, He makes even his enemies to be at peace with him."

Twenty-One

Season of Brokenness

WHILE AT CROSS City I was blessed to spend time with my kids through visitation.

Seeing and talking with my children really humbled me into a genuine process of brokenness. I couldn't explain it at the time, but I knew that something was happening on the inside of me, and I sensed that it was the Lord's doing.

Holding them in my arms was precious for me as we talked and laughed together. Though I was smiling on the outside, I was crying in my heart because I knew that I was missing out on the greatest moments of their lives. It really bothered me that I couldn't be there to participate in the early life development and spiritual orientation of my children.

My cousin Mike visited me twice while I was at Cross City. He was thrilled and assured from my conversation that I was wonderfully saved and officially in the same army as him—serving the Lord Jesus. Mike's visits reinforced a few things for me with words of wisdom concerning how to handle a few situations I was facing.

During a telephone conversation with my mother, she made a shocking statement that gripped my heart. Jennie Mae said, "Turk, Mama has some news that I have to tell you about. I have signed a will with your name on it."

I responded nervously, "Mama, what will are you talking about?"

"Baby, Mama has been on a dialysis machine too long now and my body can't take this treatment anymore." Drinking Mr. Boston liquor on the rocks ruined her liver and kidneys.

"Mama, have you made your peace with God?"

"Yeah baby."

Upon her response, immediately within, the Spirit of God revealed unto me that my mother's soul was lost and was weighing in the balance. The reality was that she wasn't saved. I had to yield to one of Jesus's effective evangelistic skills when leading lost souls to salvation. I listened to her so that I could locate where she was spiritually before I could give her the appropriate diet of the Word. This was my mother, and I wasn't going to miss it. So, I said, "Mama, how do you know that you are going to Heaven and that you have made peace with God?"

She replied, "My pastor said that God will accept me just as I am, and as long as I send my tithes I am going to Heaven."

I said, "Mama, when was the last time you saw your pastor?"

She couldn't answer me because she couldn't get out of bed two or three days at a time. She was too weak to attend church services and from what I knew, no one from her church visited her. I said, "Mama, I love you, but

I have to tell you the truth because your eternal soul is at stake. You are not saved. You must be born again. Your pastor didn't explain God's plan of salvation to you. I was honored to explain the path to salvation (*how to become saved in a relationship with God and His son Jesus Christ according to 2 Peter 3:9¹ and Romans 10:9–10²*) to my Mama.

When I explained these verses clearly to my mother concerning the plan of God's salvation for her soul, she understood. Then, I walked her through the sinner's prayer and the confession of salvation (*deliverance, freedom, and liberation in her spirit*). Upon my mother's sincere repentance and her confession of Romans 10:9–10 (*cited in footnote 71*) and Romans 10:13³ she received Jesus in her heart and her name was written in the Lamb's Book of Life as I rejoiced with the angels in Heaven.

She was crying because she felt the burden and weight of sin lifted up off her soul and spirit. I obviously shed some tears of joy as I sensed a release of God's peace overshadowing her. God blessed her to carry me nine months to birth me with a physical life and in return God blessed me to minister his word to birth her with spiritual eternal life, which is the gift of God [*John 6:63⁴; John 6:68⁵; Romans 6:23⁶; Ephesians 2:8–9⁷; John 3:3–7⁸*]

Leading my mother to the Lord Jesus was a mountaintop experience for me, and at the same time, I felt a deeper brokenness taking place within my members. I sense a part of my old man dying and yielding more over to my new spiritual inner man to be strengthened with the fullness of Christ [*2 Corinthians 5:17⁹; Ephesians 4:22–24¹⁰; 2 Corinthians 4:16¹¹; Ephesians 3:16–17¹²; Philippians 4:13¹³*]

In my season of brokenness, I began to mature in Christ as I recognized my own imperfection and inadequacies which caused me to rely on the indwelling of the Holy Spirit. I was learning to trust and depend more on the Lord because I began to acknowledge that my sufficiency and source of life is of God and not of myself. [*2 Corinthians 3:5*[14]; *Job 33:4*[15]] This was God's way of purifying my faith in him. Though my mind was made up and heart was fixed on serving the Lord, my faith was being battle-tested to be proven.

During this time, the Lord created several divine appointments for me to fellowship with certain inmates who were fallen pastors, ministers, and preachers of the Gospel in society. One by one, at different times, these redeemed men shared their hearts with me of their successes and failures in their respective churches. They expressed their strength and faithfulness, which caused them to prosper in their ministries. They shared their weaknesses and fears, which caused them to miss it and fall into sin. They spoke openly about how much pain and shame they brought upon their families as they assassinated their own characters.

From their personal experiences, they shared the dos and don'ts in ministry when serving God's people. One of the key things they all had in common was the fact that they didn't welcome being held accountable for their selfish actions or their ungodly behaviors. These humble men shared with me out of their brokenness the danger of compromising and not walking in what God had called and anointed them to do. Each of these men had missed their season in God to do great things for the Kingdom and they encouraged me not to miss mine as God raises me up.

One elderly man with whom I spent time had been a pastor of a church for twenty years, and he wasn't even saved. He couldn't even quote foundational scriptures concerning salvation; not even Romans 10:9[16]. He was in bad shape spiritually. By the grace of God, the Lord used me to explain the simplicity of the Gospel to him so that he could receive salvation. He clearly had a form of Godliness, but he wasn't walking in any Power. Once he came clean and received Jesus on the authority of God's Word, he was on his way for the Kingdom.

Though I felt I was ready to get back out into society, my second 3.800 Motion (*Motion for Correction, Reduction, and Modification of Sentence*) was denied, which added to my season of brokenness. My legal setback caused me to become more focused on the written Word [*the Bible*] to know the living Word [*Jesus*]. [*2 Timothy 3:16; John 1:1; John 1:14*] For me, the denial of my motion compelled me to reposition myself to prepare for what was to come in my walk with the Lord.

Meanwhile at Cross City, I taught and trained Christian believers in the EE classes in the Chapel. I taught the men, in a classroom setting, how to witness as a way of life, to lead the lost to Jesus. The Lord began to reveal visions to me by His Spirit that He was going to take me back to Martin C.I. to lead the lost to Christ and cast out demons in Jesus' name [*Acts 2:17*[17]; *John 16:15*[18]; *John 14:12*[19]; *Mark 16:17–20*[20]]

In my season of brokenness, I learned how to get under the authority of God's Word. I understood that in order for me to operate in Kingdom authority I must submit to the authority God has set over me. This was Jesus' secret with regard to His authority—His submission under the Father. [*Matthew 8:8–9*[21]] The centurion acknowledged this kingdom principle. By faith, with this spiritual understanding, I was empowered to do what I was called and anointed to do.

Every chance I got, I spent time in the Chapel listening to the latest Gospel music. My favorite Gospel singers are John P. Kee, the Canton Spirituals, Williams Brothers, and Shirley Caesar. The entire time that I was at Cross City, I sang second tenor in a tight Gospel quartet called, "The Sounds of Joy." We held our own as we sang for the Glory of God.

During the summer of 1998, I discovered that God had blessed me with another gift. That is, I was allowed to coordinate and direct Biblical plays from the Scriptures. The Lord used me and thirty-two other inmates in a Bible-based play in Faith Chapel called, "The Ministry of the Holy Ghost in the Early Church" from the book of Acts Chapters 5–9. These faithful men portrayed every character in these chapters with perfection, bringing the Word of God to life.

After diligently practicing and walking out the scriptures by memory for four months, Jesus was lifted up and God was glorified. That is, the inmates walked out the scriptures in a reenactment of what took place during Biblical times while wearing clothing from that era while soft, dramatic, instrumental music played in the background.

On October 10, 1998, at 6:00 p.m., an audience of 224 inmates and 21 outside guests from KAIROS Ministries were truly blessed. KAIROS means God's special time where He does a spiritual operation in the hearts of His people. KAIROS Ministries is a body of fifty to sixty unified believers from several denominations who visit prisons to share their testimonies, time, the Gospel of Christ, and most importantly, the unconditional love of God. Afterward, the Lord used me to conduct an altar call and several men responded to receive Christ. Upon successfully completing my Level IV EE training under Arthur Hallett, I was certified as a leader, teacher, and trainer in the Evangelism Explosion Ministry.

When my labor and assignment was finished at Cross City, it was confirmed unto me that it was my time to be transferred. It was a joyful moment for me to receive words of encouragement and prayer from genuine brethren whom I looked up to and respected. They held me accountable and watched over me spiritually as they helped raise me up in the Word while I was at Cross City. I gleaned, and learned the most from Ernest Atterbury, David Jones, and Bruce Downey.

On April 22, 1999, I arrived back at Martin C.I. a saved man in an old familiar place. I was reunited with

179

Woodrow Jackson and a few other men who were arrested with me in 1992. The environment at Martin C.I. was still very much violent and treacherous, but there was something different in the atmosphere. It became apparent to me that God's hand was upon Martin C.I. because the men were now more God conscious and receptive to the Word of God.

I wasn't at Martin C.I. a week before my first real test presented itself through a Jezebel spirit in an attractive female officer. She approached me in my room after she made most of the other inmates leave the dormitory. She made it known that she had heard about me, how I had it going on, and then she asked me what I wanted to do.

I told her, You got the wrong man."

She responded sarcastically, "If you are scared, say you are scared."

I replied, "The only person that I'm scared of, and reverence is God."

"What does God have to do with us?"

"Everything, because He is the one who is watching us right now."

On that note she cleared it. Just like that God showed me that the Devil doesn't care who he uses, he just needs a body to operate in.

After some quality prayer time and fasting I was led to start preaching the Gospel of Christ at the north end of the compound. My high school classmate, Jackie Clarke, rejoiced with me over the phone about my salvation in the Lord. Her brother Kenneth (*KK*), who was also doing time at Martin C.I., had given me her phone number. She was more excited for me than I was for myself because she knew how wretched I had been before my salvation.

In April 1999, Woodrow recommended to Chaplin Roger D. Lemaster that I replace him to work in the Chapel and Chaplin Lemaster hired me to do so. Woodrow was in transition to move to the work camp, so he trained me in his responsibilities in the Chapel. I was able to serve in a greater capacity by helping to maintain the order of services. I also went to the confinement areas to pray with and to witness the Gospel to lost souls. With every opportunity that presented itself, I ministered deliverance to the hurting and oppressed men who responded to the Word of God. This ministry was the vision God showed me in the spirit when I was at Cross City.

In the month of June 1999, I experienced my ultimate level of brokenness when my mother and grandmother visited me. I couldn't believe my eyes as my mother was half the size she was the last time I saw her. I fell helplessly to my knees crying as I wrapped my arms around her. I didn't care what the officers or the other visitors in the visiting park thought, this was Mama. After gathering myself together to look at her, I realized how beautiful Jennie Mae appeared with her fresh finger wave hairstyle. One of the amazing things about a mother is that no matter what she is going through in her life, she knows how to put on a poker face. Though she knew that her time and physical life were coming to an end soon, she maintained her composure and strength so she could say with a smile, "Turk, it's going to be all right, Baby." With those words she kissed me on my jaw as she patted me on the hands. The look in her eyes indicated to me that this was going to be the last time I would see her alive.

While still on my knees, I couldn't help but cry until I became exhausted. As I cried, Mama sat there peacefully with a few tears falling from her eyes, though she did not become overly emotional. Fred sat there with teary eyes and little emotion.

I hugged my mother for the whole entire visit while we talked about everything that was of importance and needed to be discussed. Then we reflected on and laughed about some fond memories we all shared together. This memorable and touching visit came to an end far too soon. I looked at my beautiful mother for the very last time. Her face was radiant, her smile was genuine, and her skin was smooth and soft. Most importantly, Jennie Mae Jolly's spirit had been born again with the assurance of knowing that to be absent from her physical body, she was going to be ushered into the presence of the Lord Jesus in Heaven (2 Corinthians 5:8[22]). I brought closure to this chapter in our lives humbly with prayer, asking and believing God for His sovereign will to be done in Jesus' name. It was difficult for me to say goodbye. I just hugged and kissed her for the very last time as I waved goodbye to her.

I began to call my mother twice a week to encourage her in the Word and pray with her. She expressed that she would love to attend church, but she was too weak to be there in person. So, I told her to tune into Channel 21 to catch Bishop T.D. Jakes.

Mama's first response after watching Bishop Jakes was, "Oooh baby, that Jake, that Jake, that Jake!"

I said, "Mama!"

She went on to say, "Baby, that man sure knows how to preach that Word. You hear me? Now, he is my kind of preacher because he talks trash as he tells it like it is."

Between myself and T.D. Jakes planting and watering the Word of God in her spirit, her faith was strengthened and built up in the Lord, which helped her to hold on.

The Lord had placed a burden on my heart to sacrifice a fast for my brother Duck's salvation and shortly thereafter he received Jesus in his heart. Duck began to bring my children to visit me because I had removed all the females from my visitation list.

On September 11, 1999, my 35th birthday, Aunt Sally Mae James passed away in South Philly. She was always sweet to me and always had warm words for me. Though she passed, she will always be in my heart, and I will always miss her dearly. Also on the same day, I was truly blessed at a four-day KAIROS weekend at the Chapel. I was surprised with a special cake for my birthday from the KAIROS Ministry who covered me in their prayers.

On October 1, 1999, the inevitable came to pass., My mother Jennie Mae Jolly passed away gracefully. This was my greatest test that took place in my Christian walk because it was a pivotal shift in my life. Upon receiving this heartbreaking news, I felt as though a sharp arrow had pierced through my heart. I was at a loss for words as my breath seemed to have left my body. My legs became weak as I felt a pull and push in the realm of the Spirit.

I had been working in the Chapel praying and comforting other inmates all the time and now I needed someone to pray me through. After Chaplin Lemaster counseled me, he told me to take off as much time as I needed to take. I left the Chapel feeling empty and with a blank mind. The Chaplin's words, and the prayers of the concerned brethren, couldn't fill the void that was left in my heart. I walked the track on the recreation field while worshipping to encourage myself in the Lord. I became a bit weary as Satan tried to shake my faith, but the Spirit of the Lord rose up within me and reminded me of God's goodness and faithfulness. God was breaking me with His love and grace.

I appreciated the body of Christ's prayers, hugs, and cards of sympathy, but it was the Word of God that filled the void that was in my heart. It was my obedience to God's Word that sustained me which enabled me to continue standing firm on my foundation in Christ. It was the Word that strengthened my wings of faith, maintaining my sanity, and keeping me from flipping out. God's Word assured me that death and the grave were defeated. They were swallowed up in victory in Jesus' resurrection.

[*1 Corinthians 15:54–57*[23]; *Matthew 28:18*[24]] The greatest provision and inheritance every born-again Christian
possesses is that sin, death, and the graveyard can't hold
us because Jesus has dominion over them and so do we
who are in Christ Jesus. [*Romans 8:12*[25]; *Romans 6:9*[26];
Revelation 1:18[27]; *Romans 8:37–39*[28]]

In the Kingdom, before God can make us, He has
to shape us on his spiritual potter's wheel to conform
us to the image of Jesus. This is exactly what the Lord
was doing in my season of brokenness. Jesus explained
this conforming process with four Kingdom principles
in Matthew 14:19[29] where He *took, blessed, broke,* and
gave to those He has called and anointed for service. Like
Joseph, Moses and King David, the Lord *took* Ma Jennie's
Boy out of his environment in society by way of his rebellious criminal lifestyle. He *blessed* me to become saved,
healed and delivered to develop my spirit in His Word. He
broke me for a season from the corruptible characteristics
of my old man's deceitful lusts and criminal behavior.
Then, He imparted His Word into my spirit so I could
give it freely to His people, the multitude, by teaching
and preaching the Gospel of Christ [*Mathew 10:1, 7–8*[30];
Acts 20:35[31]]

Had I known previously that I would have to go
through this conforming process, I would not have
matured spiritually as I did. This process also prepared
me for the passing away of my mother. My requests to
attend my mother's funeral were denied because of the
length of my prison sentence. Bless Ms. Kamala's heart
because even though I was denied, she still went far and
beyond trying to make it happen for me. In my heart I was
confident with the assurance that my mother was in a
better place, in the presence of the Lord. Moses died and

Elijah was translated and they both went to Heaven to be in the presence of the Lord. [*Deuteronomy 34:5–6*[32]; *2 Kings 2:11*[33]] For Christians, death is a departure from our physical bodies and a quick transition into Heaven in our glorious spiritual bodies. [*Philippians 3:21*[34]; *2 Corinthians 5:1–2*[35]] I'll see and recognize Ma Jennie, Sally Mae, and Jennie Mae. Her physical body that was in that casket was only a shell God blessed her to live with on this earth for fifty-three years.

In my season of brokenness, I accepted the fact that God enabled me to pass through the valley of afflictions to make me a stronger believer, a wiser servant, and a humbler person.

SIDELINE COMMENT

After my mother's funeral, I was blessed to have all my children visit me at once except my oldest son, Jeremiah. Though I enjoyed our visits I was really bothered to know that they needed me in their lives. I was fortunate to talk with all my children often over the phone. We also exchanged letters, cards, photos, "I miss you " and "I love you" with each other. It was therapeutic and comforting for me to stay connected with my children.

Acknowledging that I blew it big time with my children by not being there to assume my responsibilities toward them, I vowed before the Lord to be a Godly father on the authority of God's Word [*Deuteronomy 6:1–7*[36]; *Proverbs 22:6*[37]; *Hosea 4:6*[38]; *Proverbs 20:7*[39]; *Isaiah 44:3*[40]] Though I was bound physically in prison, it was enlightening to know that God's Word is not bound by a wall or a fence—can I get a witness! [*2 Timothy 2:9*[41]; *Isaiah 55:11*[42]]

Whenever I wrote to, or talked with, my children I always spoke into their lives with building blocks of words to help build their self-esteem. Accordingly, I had to speak to them wisely because they each had different personalities. When prayer was outlawed in public schools, I reached out immediately to teach my children that they could think prayers derived from scripture such as Ephesians 3:20.[43]

ENDNOTES

1 "The Lord is not slack concerning His promise, as some count slackness, but is longsuffering toward us, not willing that any should perish but that all should come to repentance."

2 "if you confess the Lord Jesus and believe in your heart that God has raised Him from the dead, you will be saved. For with the heart one believes unto righteousness, and with the mouth confession is made unto salvation."

3 "For 'whoever calls on the name of the Lord shall be saved.'"

4 "It is the Spirit who gives life; the flesh profits nothing. The words that I speak to you are spirit, and they are life."

5 "But Simon Peter answered Him, 'Lord, to whom shall we go? You have the words of eternal life.'"

6 "For the wages of sin is death, but the gift of God is eternal life in Christ Jesus our Lord."

7 "For by grace you have been saved through faith, and that not of yourselves; it is the gift of God, not of works, lest anyone should boast."

8 "Jesus answered and said to him, 'Most assuredly, I say to you, unless one is born again, he cannot see the kingdom of God.' Nicodemus said to Him, 'How can a man be born when he is old? Can he enter a second time into his mother's womb and be born?' Jesus answered, 'Most assuredly, I say to you, unless one is born of water and the Spirit, he cannot enter the kingdom of God. That which is born of the flesh is flesh, and that which is born of the Spirit is spirit. Do not marvel that I said to you, you must be born again.'"

9 "Therefore, if anyone is in Christ, he is a new creation; old things have passed away; behold, all things have become new."

10 "That you put off, concerning your former conduct, the old man which grows corrupt according to the deceitful lusts, and be renewed in the spirit of your mind, and that you put on the new man which was created according to God, in true righteousness and holiness."

11 "Therefore, we do not lose heart. Even though our outward man is perishing, yet the inward man is being renewed day by day."

12 "That He would grant you, according to the riches of His glory, to be strengthened with might through His Spirit in the inner man, that Christ may dwell in your hearts through faith."

13 "I can do all things through Christ who strengthens me."

14 "Not that we are sufficient of ourselves to think of anything as being from ourselves, but our sufficiency is from God."

15 "The Spirit of God has made me, And the breath of the Almighty gives me life."

16 "If you confess with your mouth the Lord Jesus and believe in your heart that God has raised Him from the dead, you will be saved."

17 "And it shall come to pass in the last days, says God, That I will pour out of My Spirit on all flesh; Your sons and your daughters shall prophesy, Your young men shall see visions, Your old men shall dream dreams."

18 "All things that the Father has are Mine. Therefore I said that He will take of Mine and declare it to you."

19 "Most assuredly, I say to you, he who believes in Me, the works that I do he will do also; and greater works than these he will do, because I go to my Father."

20 "And these signs will follow those who believe: in My name they will cast out demons; they will speak with new tongues; they will take up serpents; and if they drink anything deadly, it will by no means hurt them; they will lay hands on the sick, and they will recover. So then, after the Lord had spoken to them, He was received up into Heaven, and sat down at the right hand of God. And they went out and preached everywhere, the Lord working with them and confirming the word through the accompanying signs. Amen."

21 "The centurion answered and said, 'Lord, I am not worthy that You should come under my roof. But only speak a word, and my servant will be healed. For I also am a man under authority, having soldiers under me. And I say to this one, 'Go,' and he goes; to another, 'Come,' and he comes; and to my servant, 'Do this,' and he does it."

22 "We are confident, I say, and willing rather to be absent from the body, and to be present with the Lord."

23 "So when this corruptible has put on incorruption, and this mortal has put on immortality, then shall be brought to pass the saying that is written: 'Death is swallowed up in victory.' 'O Death, where is your sting? O Hades, where is your victory?' The sting of death is sin, and the strength of sin is the law. But thanks be to God, who gives us the victory through our Lord Jesus Christ."

24 "And Jesus came and spoke to them, saying, 'All authority has been given to Me in heaven and on earth."

25 "Therefore, brethren, we are debtors—not to the flesh, to live according to the flesh."

26 "knowing that Christ, having been raised from the dead, dies no more.

Death no longer has dominion over Him."

27 "I am He who lives, and was dead, and behold, I am alive forevermore. Amen. And I have the keys of Hades and Death."

28 "Yet in all these things we are more than conquerors through Him who loved us. For I am persuaded that neither death nor life, nor angels nor principalities nor powers, nor things present nor things to come, nor height nor depth, nor any other created thing, shall be able to separate us from the love of God which is in Christ Jesus our Lord."

29 "Then He said to them, 'Follow Me, and I will make you fishers of men.'"

30 "And when He had called His twelve disciples to Him, He gave them power over unclean spirits, to cast them out, and to heal all kinds of sickness and all kinds of disease." And as you go, preach, saying, 'The kingdom of heaven is at hand. Heal the sick, cleanse the lepers, raise the dead, cast out demons. Freely you have received, freely give.'"

31 "I have shown you in every way, by laboring like this, that you must support the weak. And remember the words of the Lord Jesus, that He said, 'It is more blessed to give than to receive.'"

32 "So Moses the servant of the Lord died there in the land of Moab, according to the word of the Lord. And He buried him in a valley in the land of Moab, opposite Beth Peor; but no one knows his grace to this day."

33 "Then it happened, as they continued on and talked, that suddenly a chariot of fire appeared with horses of fire, and separated the two of them; and Elijah went up by a whirlwind into heaven."

34 "who will transform our lowly body that it may be conformed to His glorious body, according to the working by which He is able even to subdue all things to Himself."

35 "For we know that if our earthly house, this tent, is destroyed, we have a building from God, a house not made with hands, eternal in the heavens. For in this we groan, earnestly desiring to be clothed with our habitation which is from heaven."

36 "Now this is the commandment, and these are the statutes and judgments which the LORD your God has commanded to teach you, that you may observe them in the land which you are crossing over to possess, that you may fear the LORD your God, to keep all His statutes and His commandments which I command you, you and your son and your grandson, all the days of your life, and that your days may be prolonged. Therefore hear, O Israel, and be careful to observe it, that it may be well with you, and that you may multiply greatly as the LORD God of your fathers has promised you—'a land flowing with milk and honey.' Hear, O Israel: The LORD our God, the LORD is one! You shall love the LORD your God with all your heart, with all your soul, and with all your strength. And these words which I command you today shall be in your heart. You shall teach them diligently to your children, and shall talk of them when you sit in your house, when you

walk by the way, when you lie down, and when you rise up."

37 "Train up a child in the way he should go, And when he is old he will not depart from it."

38 "My people are destroyed for lack of knowledge. Because you have rejected knowledge, I also will reject you from being priest for Me; Because you have forgotten the law of your God, I also will forget your children."

39 "The righteous man walks in his integrity; His children are blessed after him."

40 "For I will pour water on him who is thirsty, And floods on the dry ground; I will pour My Spirit on your descendants, And My blessing on your offspring."

41 "for which I suffer trouble as an evildoer, even to the point of chains; but the word of God is not chained."

42 "So shall My word be that goes forth from My mouth; It shall not return to Me void, But it shall accomplish what I please, And it shall prosper in the thing for which I sent it."

43 "Now to Him who is able to do exceedingly abundantly above all that we ask or think, according to the power that works in us."

Twenty-Two

Promotion in the Kingdom

A FEW WEEKS after my mother's funeral I had a dangerous confrontation with a gang leader in the Chapel. This
individual had the audacity to try and cut a drug deal in
the sanctuary. As soon as I recognized the move I confronted and rebuked that spirit in Jesus' name, telling
him to cease his illegal activity in God's house. He got very
upset and threatened to kill me when he caught up with
me on the compound. Then, he said he was going to see
if Jesus was going to save me. My blood pressure shot up
and the old me wanted to take the crime to him, but the
Holy Spirit reminded me that I wasn't dealing with flesh
and blood. I identified with that drug dealing spirit that
had him bound because it was the same spirit that once
trolled me and influenced my past actions and behavior. Accordingly, I didn't take this threat lightly because
when a convict at Martin C.I. announces his intent to
kill somebody, it's on. Serving the Lord on the front-line

invites trouble and confrontation with the enemy. This is what Jesus, Paul, and the Psalmist meant in John 16:33,[1] 2 Timothy 3:12,[2] and Psalm 46:1,[3] respectively.

Someone was going to die or get seriously injured. I had to literally lay on the altar and pray, asking God for His help, peace, guidance, and words of wisdom to deal with this hurting and lost soul. My homeboy, Dennis Carter (*D.C.*) witnessed what happened, as he was working in the Chapel also. When I left the Chapel, I went straight to the gang leader's dorm. D.C. happened to live in the same quad with him in that dorm. D.C. was unsuccessful in attempting to stop me from going into their quad. Though I was entering into a death trap, I wasn't going in my own strength. I was going prayerfully in the name of the Lord.

When I confronted the gang leader, as his followers stood by, I expressed the exact words God placed in my Spirit to speak to him. He acknowledged what I said without saying a word and then I left without a physical altercation popping off. Thank God for His Word because the "Good Book" says, A soft answer turns away wrath" (*Proverbs 15:1*).

The next day the gang leader came to me with my Uncle Bean who was also at Martin C.I. He came to apologize, stating that he was wrong. He also let me know that him and Bean were tight and that he didn't know I was Bean's nephew. He also expressed that he was sorry to hear about my mother's passing and that if I needed anything to just let him know.

As the new millennium approached, the media and the entire world were caught in an uproar over some wannabe's prediction that the world was going to end on December 31, 1999, at 11:59:59. Even my children were caught up in the pandemonium. I assured Adam Jr. and Candee that Jesus said, "But of that day and hour no one knows, not even the angels of heaven, but my Father only" (*Matthew 24:36*). When January 1, 2000 rolled in, people gladly got their lives back to normal.

On February 2, 2000, we had the NFL's Tampa Buccaneers' Coach, Tony Dungy, come out with Abe Brown's prison ministry for one of our Black History programs. After the service, Tony fielded questions about his Christian walk and his NFL playing days and coaching experiences. I asked him to share with us his sideline view of Barry Sanders' shake and bake moves as he ran through his Bucs defense. He said he couldn't put Barry's artistic running style into words because it was unexplainable, ridiculous, and just purely magical.

For Easter 2000, the Lord blessed me with His favor to conduct, direct, and present Martin C.I.'s first Easter Ministry play. With thirty-two faithful inmates, we brought God's Word to life in every character from the passages in Matthew Chapters 26–28.

After four months of walking through fun and focused practices, Martin C.I. administration, inmate population, and outside ministries were truly blessed when they saw Jesus' ministry, death, burial, and resurrection re-enacted before their very eyes. God saturated the atmosphere in the Chapel with His anointed presence which magnified what we did for His glory and honor.

Because there was a daring escape by helicopter from the Jimmy Rice Facility adjacent to Martin C.I., I was transferred on July 1, 2000, to Desoto C.I. to help renovate another Jimmy Rice Facility with my A/C and Heating skills. It took only a one-hour-and-twenty-minute drive west on Highways 27 and 70 to get to my destination. This was D.O.C.'s plan but God had another plan and purpose in mind for Ma Jennie's boy.

Arriving at Desoto C.I., I made my calling and election sure by devoting myself to a two-day fast and prayer to seek God's will and direction. God confirmed my promotion in His Kingdom. I knew in my Spirit that my elevation to another dimension in the Kingdom came from God and not man. [*Psalm 75:6 – 7*[4]; *Acts 13:21 – 22*[5]]

The Greek word for "kingdom" is Basileia which signifies God's Heavenly and Royal dominion in which He rules in the lives of Christians while they are on this earth. I knew that by His Spirit and divine Power, God was going to empower me to accomplish the labor He had in store for me. [*Zechariah 4:6*[6]; *2 Peter 1:3 – 4*[7]; *Daniel 11:32*[8]

The Spirit of God enabled me to see into the realm of the Spirit to visualize my assignment and purpose in the body of Christ and know my mission with the lost men at Desoto C.I. In my first Chapel service I was asked to introduce myself and share my testimony. I responded with, "My name is Adam Jolly. The brethren call me Brother Jolly. I am saved, Christ is the head of my life and I love the Lord. I came from Martin C.I. and I didn't ask to come here. I was requested by D.O.C. but chosen and beckoned by God to be at Desoto for such a time as this. I believe in laying hands on the sick, I speak in tongues, I don't mind slanging the blood of Jesus, and I believe in casting demons out of oppressed people, in the name of Jesus, who are bound by Satan. I hate the Devil and he hates me and everything that God loves. I have come to tear down the Devil's kingdom and advance God's Kingdom in the hearts of men, one soul at a time from the inside out with the Word of God. *Can you say 'Amen'?*"

My testimony served notice to the body of Christ and to the enemy as to where I stood. The religious crown and the carnally minded put a bull's eye on Ma Jennie's boy.

After the service, the first genuine brother I got acquainted with was a Haitian named Julien. Despite the fact that Julien was going through a physical Job-like experience with his skin, I was one of the very few who truly embraced him without looking at him crazy. This meant a lot to him because the brethren who had already been there for years had distanced themselves from him. We cut a covenant relationship like that of David and Jonathan as he became a spiritual son to me. It was Julien who introduced me to the front-line soldiers and generals in the faith at Desoto.

When I shared my testimony and spoke with the head of the Recreation (*Rec*) Department, I received his approval to establish the Recreation Field Ministry God had equipped me to perfect. Every Friday from 1:00 – 3:00 p.m., I preached the Gospel of Christ to lost souls on the rec. field during rain, winter, or sunshine. Making full proof of my evangelistic ministry, I demonstrated my office in the faith by leading lost souls to Christ and ministering deliverance to the hurting and oppressed.

Before I was proven and released to minister to the body of Christ, Julien pulled my coat to inform me that the leaders felt threatened by the presence of God's anointing upon my life. To get more acquainted with me, they invited me to their weekly board meeting. One by one, they introduced themselves: Carlos, Kelly, Sanders, Miguel, Peter, Julien, June, and Banks. Observing them quietly as they talked, it became clearer to me why God positioned me strategically at Desoto with His Kingdom assignment.

After the meeting, Carlos asked me what I thought about what was discussed concerning the things of God and the ministry. I said, "I heard what was not said." Kelly said, "What do you mean Brother Jolly?"

I said, Brethren, James said to be swift to hear and slow to speak. [*James 1:19*] I heard everything that was said but I didn't hear book, chapter, and verse by the

Spirit to validate what was discussed concerning God's Kingdom business. For us to expect a great move of God by His Spirit, we can't mix spirituality with carnality. In other words, if we really want God to bless what we do for His Kingdom, it's paramount that we align ourselves with His Word. God and His Word are one. Therefore, He is obligated with an oath to honor His Word in the lives of His anointed ambassadors who teach and preach the Gospel of Christ. Hence, there must be a Biblical order for the leadership of the Holy Spirit to flow liberally, so that the Word of the Lord may have free course.

Lastly, I said, "God desires that one of you become the appointed spiritual leader of the ministry." I explained that God has always used leaders such as Abraham, Joseph, Moses, and Joshua to guide and speak to His people. After I spoke, they all had something to say. They were all basically in agreement with each other to keep their ministry status quo, without appointing a leader.

My concluding words were, "I didn't come to be that appointed leader. I'm here to submit to God's sovereign will and to help enhance what He wants to do through the Body of Christ. My heart's desire is that we align ourselves with the Word of God so that we can elevate to another dimension in the Kingdom together. By the Spirit of the Lord, God will confirm His Word I have spoken to you all."

My concluding remarks were followed by a closing prayer, and we went our separate ways to our dormitories for count time.

I announce to you that it only took God a few hours to confirm His Word that same night. The very next morning during work call at the center gate, Banks and Sanders were waiting on me anxiously to share the praise report. Sanders explained that after the board meeting, he received a letter from his brother in the dorm. Sanders said, "Brother Jolly, my brother is a pastor. God just used him to confirm what you shared with us last night." He said God told him to tell me, "Now is the time for the brethren at Desoto to align themselves with the Word of God and appoint a qualified, seasoned leader over the Body of Christ. It's God's divine order and will for His people."

James Sanders and Jeffrey Banks lived in the same dorm, so they were the only two who knew of the confirmed report.

Walking in my promotion in the Kingdom, the Spirit of the Lord had elevated my thinking to make wise and sound decisions concerning the things of God. So, I wisely told Sanders and Banks to keep this inside Kingdom information in their hearts until God's appointed time. The vision and the work were too great to release this information onto the ears of carnal believers who couldn't see spiritually and who refused to respond to God's voice because of the religion and tradition in which they were entrenched.

In my Christian walk I learned that I couldn't go with God spiritually if I stayed where I was—unlearned in His Word and undeveloped in my Spirit. The prophet Nehemiah said, "I told no one what my God had put in my heart to do at Jerusalem" (*Nehemiah 2:12*).

Because of the carnal people who were prideful and fearful, God told Gideon, "Then it will be, that of whom I say to you, 'This one shall go with you,' the same shall go with you; and of whomsoever I say to you, 'This one shall not go with you,' the same shall not go" (*Judges 7:4*).

I shared with Sanders and Banks that a percentage of the brethren aren't where they think they are spiritually. It was going to take a little time for them to elevate their faith in the Word of God because only a few were prepared to go forth. Meanwhile, they were admonished that we have to be careful how we embark upon sharing the Lord's Word and they agreed.

The "Table of Fire" was the name of the compound ministry in which they had established a bilingual service amongst the inmate population. Every Saturday morning from 8:00 – 11:00 a.m., an average of forty to fifty Spanish and English believers came together to fellowship in the Lord. When Julien's date came up in the preaching rotation, he motioned to the board that I go forth in his place. There was a little resistance initially from the undesirable, but the majority seconded the motion in favor of releasing me to minister in his stead.

The first message I ministered I titled, "Willing to Justify," was a word God confirmed from the text in *Luke 10:25 – 30* [the parable of the Good Samaritan]. A few days before I preached, Julien said, "Brother Jolly, a lot of men have gone and God hadn't sent them, but you, I know in my Spirit that God sent you here to do something special in the Body. He then gave me book, chapter, and verse from Jeremiah 14:14,[9] 23:21,[10] and 27:15.[11] When the hour came for Ma Jennie's boy to preach the Word, it was on as the anointing of God's Holy Ghost Power rested on me. Julien enjoyed every second as the Lord used me to minister the revelation of God's Word with principal applications.

This bilingual ministry was a unique blessing for me because it really helped me train and develop my speech delivery when ministering being that I'm a Nassau

(*Bahamian*), I had a bad habit of talking too fast when I got excited about Jesus. In this ministry I had to wait for the sentence. That is, I spoke to be interpreted before I could continue on with the next spoken word. This was a challenging transition for me, but the Spirit of the Lord strengthened me to harness my gift to minister more effectively while operating in my promotion of the Kingdom. I discovered that clothing myself with humility is a wonderful virtue. It assured me that people couldn't knock, or bring me down, because I didn't exalt myself in the first place.

My cousin Mike visited me twice to inform me about what was going on with the family and how the Lord was blessing him. I was blessed to see most of my children while I was at Desoto. One of the things that surprised me the most, besides my kids' growth, was how fast Adam, Jr. could run. During visitation I would always spot my son five yards outside the visiting Park Area and I'd outrun him with ease. However, on one particular visit, the boy at the age of eleven had some unusual spring in his stride. I realized quickly that I couldn't spot him anymore, so we lined up evenly and took off. After ten yards I pulled up with a fake hamstring injury because my son was blowing my doors. I wasn't going to embarrass myself as the other visitors were watching. It was too late though because the visitors were laughing as they watched us.

Though Fred and Tiny visited several times, when I called home, Tiny began to threaten me that if

I mentioned the name of Jesus, she was going to hang up on me and I would tell her, "If you do, I will call right back." Every chance I got I plugged in Jesus until God gave me more wisdom and grace to season my words with salt as I witnessed to my family.

On January 25, 2001, my friend and elderly mother in the Lord, Mrs. Louise Matheny, passed away. She always prayed with me, asking God for my salvation. She saw the gift and calling of God upon my life when I didn't see it. Now, I'm experiencing what she saw, and I understand what she was talking about concerning the goodness of the Lord. I knew she was proud of me because I finally stopped selling drugs and started serving the Lord.

Meanwhile at Desoto, I learned how to bake in the culinary arts program, which was a blessing. My favorite dish, which I loved to bake, was pineapple upside down cake.

After one of our Chapel services, I heard someone asking, "Who is Brother Jolly?" I turned around to see a brother in the Lord named James Brown who was 6-foot 5-inches tall and who weighed 280 pounds, and he definitely wasn't the "Godfather of Soul." He said, "Man of God, I heard about you in North Florida; how the Lord is using you in the Kingdom. I want you to know that I believe in laying on of hands, speaking in tongues, and putting that Devil to flight. I got your back and I'm here to labor with you in the Lord."

A few weeks later, this Vanilla Ice popping White brother named David Spikes came on the scene to join

spiritual forces with us also. When Spikes first arrived
at Desoto, he acknowledged my evangelistic ministry on
the Rec. Field and desired to preach but he didn't know
how to approach me. One night after a service, he stopped
me in the flesh and said boldly, "Brother Jolly you aren't
the only one that God has called to preach the Gospel of
Christ." I looked at Spikes and said, "Joker, you need to sit
down somewhere." When he humbled his ego and flesh to
submit to what God was doing, I took him under my wing
and nurtured him in the Word of God slowly and wisely.

When Spikes understood that he had to pay a spiritual
price to operate under the residential anointing I was
flowing in, he passed the first critical test. Once Spikes
proved himself and endured a season of growing and
being mentored in the Word, I began to release him to
preach the Gospel of Christ out on the Rec. Field.

It was a strange sight to see a shirtless White dude
preaching the Gospel to a predominantly Black captive
audience. God knew what He was doing, and I had enough
Spiritual sense to not get in the way of God's sovereign
will being done. Spikes brought a different dynamic flavor
to the Rec. Field ministry which was effective as more
souls came into the Kingdom.

My homeboy, Kinser Brown (*K.B.*) from Martin County
arrived at Desoto. I didn't recognize who he was until he
recalled how I used to roll and how he used to come to my
parties up in the yard on Tarpon with his partner, Tracy
Stewart. I responded, "Man, I'm saved now. Turk is dead.
I had to bury that joker on November 17, 1996."

K.B. replied, "Man, I heard about you being saved.
Everybody is saved."

"I don't know what you're talking about. I believed and
confessed that Jesus died and was buried and resurrected

for me. I don't know about everybody else, but based upon the authority of God's Word, I'm wonderfully saved."

K.B. said, "Okay man," as he looked at me with a little uncertainty.

A few days later, K.B. witnessed me preaching on the Rec. Field about the rich man and Lazarus from Luke 16:19–34. Two weeks later, K.B. received Jesus into his heart as his personal Lord and Savior. Upon K.B. receiving salvation, I met his mother and fiancé, Mrs. Delia and Wallesia, respectively, in the visiting park when he shared the wonderful news that he was saved.

When Mrs. Delia saw me she asked me, "Do you know who I am?"

I said, "No ma'am."

Then she said, "I know who you are, you robbed them people."

"Yes ma'am, I did rob them people."

She was referring to those 1982 robberies I committed with Harry and Mickey in Tallahassee and Panama City. While I did not know Mrs. Delia, our encounter reflected the reality of Numbers 32:23 which states in pertinent part, ". . . you have sinned against the LORD; and be sure your sin will find you out." After our visitation, and before our visitors left, K.B. asked me to pray for his mother and family, at which time Mrs. Delia and Wallesia became my mother, sister, and friends in the Lord.

God spoke to my heart to inform the ministry leaders to cast lots without nominating themselves, and the official leader would be appointed by God. By a 7–2 margin, Jeffrey Banks was established as the leader of the Table of Fire ministry. Under Banks' leadership by the Spirit of the Lord, we began to do a monumental work in the Kingdom as God released His yoke-destroying anointing.

We had vowed to fast before God, with a Kingdom purpose, for His divine guidance and direction. This was a season of maturing for all of us in our promotion in the Kingdom.

Often our fasting would occur on fried chicken day, which was D.O.C.'s best meal, so you know that it was a challenging season for us to discipline our flesh to position ourselves. As a direct result of our obedience, lives were transformed by the power of God's Word as men received Christ and their deliverance.

One day, out of nowhere, I came under attack by Satan as my back went out completely. For a whole week I was in serious pain as I walked bowed down and couldn't straighten up. When I decided to check into the infirmary, the Holy Spirit convicted me and said, "Where is your faith? You are the one who has been laying hands on the sick, believing God for their healing. I said, 'Okay Lord.'" I had Pastor Banks call an urgent meeting for the leaders and elders in the faith. When everyone arrived, I explained my back problem, then I said, "If anyone of you are living in sin or are bound in any known sin, please don't put your filthy hands on Ma Jennie's boy." Upon that announcement several men walked away as Banks, Julien, J.B., Carlos, Peter, and Sanders laid their hands on me with the prayer of faith according to James 5:14 – 15.[12] After they prayed in Jesus' name, I said, "I got it." By faith I received my healing as I walked away still partially bent over, rejoicing in the Lord. The next morning, to the

Glory of God, I woke up with a totally restored and pain-free back.

In the month of May 2001, during my prayer time, the Lord spoke to my heart to put on a play entitled the "Ministry of the Holy Ghost in the Early Church" in the Chapel. With Chaplain Lannigan and Warden Kings' approval, in the month of August 2001, thirty-two faithful men presented the first showing of the play to Region IV D.O.C. Director Martha Villacorta, Assistant Regional Director David Harris and forty other D.O.C. department head leaders. They were truly blessed by the costumes and sound effects as the Lord used us to bring His World to life from Acts 5:9 – 20 (*about God's judgment, miracles, and signs and wonders in the early church*). We then presented the play to the inmate population, and they too were blessed by the ministry.

I will never forget where I was and what I was doing on my 37th birthday and neither will you. It was 8:46 a.m. on September 11, 2001. I was at Desoto C.I. on my bunk in Sergeant Crenshaw's dorm, relaxing and reading my Bible. As I spoke a silent prayer, I didn't know that over 3,000 people would die on my birthday. 9/11 will be remembered forever and one day will become a national memorial day.

Following the Lord's lead, I contacted Arthur Hallett to ask him to come to Desoto to help me establish the EE Ministry there. On March 31, 2002, the Lord used thirty-two inmates and myself to present the Easter Ministry play in the Chapel, which was a blessing to those in attendance from the administration and the inmate population.

After completing my assigned mission at Desoto, I wanted to go to South Bay C.I. where Wine Head was, but a vision from the Lord and a letter from Chaplain Lemaster the same week confirmed that Martin C.I. was my next destination.

A day before leaving, I had an unexpected meeting with all the ministers of the Gospel. Upon breaking the news that I was transferring the next morning they were all surprised and began to shed tears of joy. One by one they expressed how they were blessed by my evangelistic calling and how they would miss my fellowship in the Lord. After expressing their love and encouraging words, Banks prayed.

On July 1, 2000, after twenty-four months, I was transferred back to Martin C.I.

ENDNOTES

1 "These things I have spoken to you, that in Me you may have peace. In the world you will have tribulation; but be of good cheer, I have overcome the world."

2 "Yes, and all who desire to live godly in Christ Jesus will suffer persecution."

3 "God is our refuge and strength, A very present help in trouble."

4 "For exaltation comes neither from the east Nor from the west nor from the south. "But God is the Judge: He puts down one, And exalts another."

5 And afterward they asked for a king; so God gave them Saul the son of Kish, a man of the tribe of Benjamin, for forty years. And when He had removed him, He raised up for them David as king, to whom also He gave testimony and said, 'I have found David the son of Jesse, a man after My own heart, who will do all My will.'"

6 "So he answered and said to me: This is the word of the Lord to Zerubbabel: 'Not by might nor by power, but by My Spirit,' Says the Lord of hosts."

7 "As His divine power has given to us all things that pertain to life and godliness, through the knowledge of Him who called us by glory and virtue, by which have been given to us exceedingly great and precious promises, that through these you may be partakers of the divine nature, having escaped the corruption that is in the world through lust."

8 "Those who do wickedly against the covenant he shall corrupt with flattery; but the people who know their God shall be strong, and carry out great exploits."

9 "And the LORD said to me, 'The prophets prophecy lies in My name. I have not sent them, commanded them, nor spoken to them; they prophesy to you a false vision, divination, a worthless thing, and the deceit of their heart.'"

10 "I have not sent these prophets, yet they ran. I have not spoken to them, yet they prophesied."

11 "'for I have not sent them,' says the LORD, 'yet they prophesy a lie in My name, that I may drive you out, and that you may perish, you and the prophets who prophesy to you.'"

12 "Is anyone among you sick? Let him call for the elders of the church, and let them pray over him, anointing him with oil in the name of the Lord. And the prayer of faith will save the sick, and the Lord will raise him up. And if he has committed sins, he will be forgiven."

Twenty-Three

God's Plan of Salvation

ON JULY 2, 2002, I arrived back at Martin C.I. with a fresh anointing to embark upon a new assignment. The Body of Christ was thrilled to see me, while at the same time, the enemy with his crowd was irritated and hated to see my return. Chaplain Lemaster had me reassigned to the Chapel where I assumed my prior responsibilities. Working in the Chapel is where I learned how to relate to and understand Muslims, Hebrew Israelites, and every other religion that opposes Jesus Christ and the Word of God.

For the record, Christianity is not a religion, it is a daily experience in a wonderful, Holy, and righteous relationship with God through Jesus Christ. From the beginning, in Genesis, God has always required a blood sacrifice for the atonement of his people. The word atonement means forgiveness, pardon, cleansing, restoration, and reconciliation. Every born-again Christian can boldly say what no one in any other religion in the world can say. That is, Jesus Christ is our blood sacrifice that has made provision for us to receive atonement. [Romans 5:8 – 11[1]] God is no respecter of persons, which is why He said, "Whosoever believes in Him [Jesus] should not perish, but have everlasting life" (*John 3:16[2]*). If you have not repented (*turned away*) from your sins and received Jesus Christ in your heart, sir, ma'am, son, daughter, brother, sister, you are that "whosoever". Jesus not only came to save and deliver us from our condition of sin, but He came to take away the state of our sin problem. [*Matthew 1:21[3]; John 1:29[4]*] Humanity inherited its sinful nature from Adam's disobedience, but thank God by Jesus' obedience Christian believers are made and clothed in the Lord's righteousness (*right standing with God*). [*Romans 5:19[5]*] Sin means to miss the mark, to err, and to trespass. [*Matthew 22:29[6]; Ephesians 2:1[7]*] Sin is that thing and consciousness in our flesh that's always lurking to potentially influence us to do the wrong thing or be unrighteous. [*James 4:17[8]; Romans 3:20[9]; 1 John 3:4[10]; 1 John 5:17[11]*] For Christian believers, when we sin we miss the mark, but God has already made provision for us to get back into right standing with Him through our obedience to His Word. [*1 John 1:9[12]*] When any Christian sins, we have an advocate (*the best lawyer in Jesus to represent us*) with the Father. [*1 John 2:1[13]*]

If you aren't saved, you need to understand that Jesus is not only the appropriation (*atonement and substitution*) for the sins of Christians. Jesus is also the atonement and substitution for the sins of the whole world (*every unsaved person including you, yes even you*). [*1 John 2:2[14]; 1 John 2:4 – 10[15]*] You have to respond in obedience by saying "yes" to God's Word and will for your life. God's love and forgiveness is greater than any sin. When you repent and forsake sin, the power of God is present and will enter your heart to help you. Our eternal destiny depends on our decision concerning Jesus. In fact, what you believe right now not only governs how you live today, but it determines where you will spend eternity.

Since I accepted and allowed Jesus into my heart on November 17, 1996, I haven't regretted one day of being saved. I've learned in the scriptures not to look down on others, thinking that I'm better than they are, or to oppress anybody because I was once lost and bound in sin. [*Exodus 22:9*[16], *21–22*[17]; *1 Corinthians 10:12*[18]; *Galations 6:3*[19]]

When God saved and delivered me, He took away my corrupted heart and gave me a heart of compassion for His people. [*Ezekiel 36:26*[20]] Compassion speaks to a deep yearning that responds to the needs of people. It was compassion that compelled and moved Jesus to heal the sick and go to the cross for us. [*Matthew 14:14*[21]; *Mark 1:40–42*[22]; *Matthew 27:39–42*[23]] Had Jesus come off the cross, God's plan of Salvation wouldn't have come to fruition, and you wouldn't be reading the Bible or this book.

From the very beginning, after Adam's fall, God designed a Kingdom master plan to reconcile humanity back unto Himself through Jesus. Salvation means to be saved, delivered, preserved, healed, and rescued. It also means safety from the power and penalty of sin. Salvation also means to experience presently God's power of deliverance which enables us to walk in liberty.

Salvation doesn't supersede the Word of God. This is why the Gospel of Christ must be preached under the Anointing before a person can receive salvation. [*Acts 4:12*[24]; *Romans 1:16*[25]; *Romans 10:9*[26]; *2 Peter 3:9*[27]; *1 Timothy 2:3–6*[28]]

Meanwhile, working in the Chapel, visiting the confinement area, and preaching on the Rec. field taught me, personally, how to be effective and victorious in spiritual warfare. In other words, as a minister of the Gospel, it's paramount that I know that Jesus who is in me is greater than the Devil and his demons who are in the world. [*John 4:4*[29]] Under the Anointing I would inform the unsaved and hurting men that they were bound and oppressed by a real enemy and not the White man or the police. That is, they were bound and oppressed by the Devil, otherwise known as Satan. [*Luke 13:16*[30]; *Acts 10:38*[31]; *2 Timothy 2:26*[32]] I would then let them know that only Jesus could set them free spiritually through the truth of God's Word, their faith and by worshiping the Lord Jesus. Jesus healed the woman with the issue of blood. [*John 8:32*[33], *36*[34]; *Mark 5:25–34*] Jesus healed blind Bartimaeus. [*Mark 10:46–52*]

Most of the men didn't care to hear the Gospel being preached on the Rec. Field every Friday morning, and some were outright mad and as irritated as a junk-yard dog. Those involved in every religion outside of Christianity that opposed Jesus and the Word of God definitely couldn't stand to hear the preaching of the cross. The officers didn't know what to expect as I preached to a captive audience of four to five hundred inmates. This was a gated community, an audience of killers, murderers, rapists, robbers, thugs, gang members, and every other type of criminal outcast from society. In addition to dying and being buried for the ungodly and sinners, Jesus got up to justify whosoever believes in Him before God—that's the Gospel. [*Romans 5:6*[35], *8*[36]; *1 Corinthians 15:3–4*[37]; *Romans 4:24–25*[38]]

While I preached, the officers heard their diet of the Word also. Good thing they were present because, if some of the inmates had AK-47 assault rifles or handguns they would have gunned me down as well as a few faithful brethren with me, for preaching and singing Gospel songs to usher in God's presence which saturated the atmosphere with His yoke-destroying anointing. I patterned my calling and evangelistic ministry after those of Billy Graham and R. W. Shambach. That is, I patterned my ministry after Billy Graham's total dedication to the call of soul winning and after R. W. Shambach's bold preaching.

I never worried about anyone doing harm to Ma Jennie's boy because I knew who was on my side. [*Romans 8:31*[39]; *Psalms 124:1–2*[40]; *Isaiah 54:15*[41]; *17*[42]] Before every message I preached, I allowed the Spirit of the Lord to confirm God's Word before I went forth. The Lord always confirmed His Word with signs and wonders as I preached His Word faithfully. [*John 14:12*[43]; *Mark 16:17*[44], *20*[45]] As the Holy Ghost and conviction fell upon the hearts of men who heard the Gospel, they responded to the drawing of God's Spirit for salvation. [*Acts 2:37*[46]; *16:30–31*[47]; *10:44*[48]; *John 6:44*[49]] Like Moses, I told God that if His presence didn't go before me and with me, I wouldn't preach the Gospel. [*Exodus 33:15*[50]]

During a visit with my classmate, Jackie, I also spoke with my oldest daughter, Yashekia, and my youngest daughter, Turquoise (Q). It was wonderful to see them both, but Q was really defiant, open, and honest concerning how she felt about me. Her mother had to actually order her to go outside the visiting area to talk with me. It was a father's sobering moment as my little princess expressed her hurting heart to me. She was only six months old when I left and now she was twelve. While she talked, I listened and prayed, asking God for a word of wisdom for her. Q was not only my youngest daughter, but I sensed that she was the smartest intellectually of all my kids. This girl was a whiz kid who was sharp with her words. I concluded our conversation by apologizing for the pain and void I caused in her life. Then I let her know that I respected her feelings and assured her of my love and concern for her.

Yashekia and I had made an agreement during her senior year in high school, but she reneged on me and I haven't heard from her since. Adam, Jr. was not sociable and never really had too much to say when he visited me. It really began to bother my son to know that I couldn't leave with him, after he visited with me, and be the father he so desperately needed in his life. As with all my children, I expressed my love and concern to Adam, Jr. every chance I got. In the end, his mother and I decided to make it optional for him to visit me.

Like Job, I sanctified my children in prayer daily by pleading the blood of Jesus over them for His divine protection. [*Job 1:5*[51]]

Growing up we've all said things in our hearts and did things we shouldn't have done — can I get a witness?

How many know that you've got to turn your plate over to see the manifestation of God's power. When you know how to do spiritual warfare in the Heavenlies, God will make the Devil back up off your loved ones. [*Matthew 16:18–20*[52]; *Joshua 23:10*[53]; *Luke 10:17–20*[54]]

In *Luke 10:17 and Mark 16:17*[55] Jesus' name is the key for Christians who operate in Kingdom authority. All power in heaven and in earth is in the name of Jesus. This same resurrection power has been delegated unto the Church, also known as the Body of Believers. [*Matthew 28:18*[56]; *Philippians 2:10*[57]; *Ephesians 1:22*[58]; *Colossians 1:18*[59]; *Acts 1:18*[60], *4:31*[61], *33*[62]]

In March 2003, I contacted Arthur Hallett in St. Petersburg, Florida to come to Martin C.I. to assist me in establishing the EE Ministry. Mr. and Mrs. Charlie and Louise Rozzell came in weekly from Ft. Lauderdale to oversee as I taught and trained the men to be soul winners. Twice a year, every six months, Arthur would come to conduct a graduation and present certificates to the men.

On May 17–18, 2003, a two-day tent revival was held on the Rec. Field under Pastor Paul Smith's leadership. Reverend Harrison Freeman of Lighthouse Baptist Church, Port St. Lucie, Florida, and Pastor Jonathan McClain of Abundant Life Ministries of Stuart blessed everyone with their praise and worship ministries. Myself, Michael Cooper (*ex-convict*), and Woodrow Jackson (*ex-convict*) were the featured ministers who preached the Gospel of Christ. One hundred and twenty-five men responded by receiving Christ as their personal Lord and Savior.

D.O.C. Region IV Chaplain Franklin Smith and the Stuart News's very own Jeff Brumley and Deborah Silver were on hand to witness this move of God at Martin C.I.

The following week, Chaplain Daniel and the Assistant Warden, Mr. Inman, gave me approval to teach a new believers' discipleship class for the new converts every Wednesday morning in the Chapel sanctuary. It was a blessing and a humbling experience for me to not only see the fruit from the revival I labored in, but also to be favored to teach and help develop the Spirits of these men with the Word of God.

It was an honor to be part of God's plan of salvation which advances His Kingdom in the hearts of His people. During February 2004, Assistant Warden Inman came to the Chapel and handed me the keys to the administration's staff canteen. He said the job was mine if I wanted it. I thanked Mr. Inman first, then he requested stipulations before I could accept the job. Because this seventy-dollar-a-month job was time consuming and would have restricted my involvement in the ministries God had ordained for me, I declined the job and returned the keys to Mr. Inman.

On April 9, 2004, we presented the Easter Ministry play in the Chapel for the administration, different outside church ministries and the inmate population. We were blessed with Biblical costumes from Dr. D. James Kennedy Ministries which enhanced the performance for the Glory of God.

On December 12, 2004, Pastor Henry Lewis passed away. He pastored Macedonia Baptist Church in East Stuart where I had become God conscious. During a conversation with my cousin Michael over the weekend of Pastor Lewis' funeral, he told me that I was the topic of conversation after the funeral. I said at the funeral, "How did that come about?" He said that I was in the center of a photo in the obituary with Pastor Lewis and the Church deacons. Someone recognized me and conversation about me blew up from there.

It was Ma Jennie who made me rejoin Macedonia Church and choir when I was released from Martin C.I. in January 1987. However, it was Pastor Lewis who had me taking up the offering for those who were sick and or poor. It was Pastor Lewis who took me to pastoral conferences with him and his deacons. The photo in the obituary had been taken at one of those conferences. Though I wasn't saved and looked the part of a minister, it was God's divine purpose, Pastor Lewis' sincere intention and Ma Jennie's heart's desire to keep me in the ark of safety. Looking back, I acknowledge that God had me covered, which shielded my life from being taken by the Devil.

As I was exposed to the church environment around Pastor Lewis during that season, certain things were imparted to me that still benefit me today. Pastor Lewis rests in peace in the presence of the Lord and he is still missed greatly. Mrs. Willie Mae Johnson sent me Pastor Lewis' obituary, he was her brother. She also informed me that she stayed under the blood of Jesus as Hurricane Katrina passed over and it did no harm to her home. She then encouraged me to stay under the blood of Jesus.

In February 2005, after the New England Patriots defeated the Philadelphia Eagles in the Super Bowl, my faith was tried again by another Jezebel spirit in a sweet smelling, attractive female officer. Early on this particular morning while inmates were still asleep, I sensed the presence of someone else in my single man room. When I opened my eyes, there she was posted up beside my bed, staring at me in the dark. Since it was very cold and the heating system was not good, I was buried under three blankets dressed in my thermals. I thought I was dreaming for a moment until she started smiling and asked, "What's up?"

I responded by also asking, "What's up? What are you doing in here and cut that light on."

She then said, "Oh, the Sergeant sent me to ask you for a scripture." I shut that deceptive move down quickly as I advised her to get out of my room and told her that I was going to speak with her and the Sergeant the following day. A lying spirit doesn't care who tells its lies. The Devil just needs a willing body in which to operate. I could have easily gotten my groove on with her without anyone knowing about it, but I chose wisely to maintain my anointing and my integrity before God.

I had been incarcerated for thirteen years and was a virgin in the Lord, having been saved, for eight of those thirteen years. I understood clearly that God is omnipresent [*everywhere at all times*] (*Psalms 139:7*,[63] *Proverbs 15:3*,[64] and *Hebrews 4:13*[65]). I was proud of myself for passing that test because I understood that if God didn't allow for me to be tested, He couldn't bless me.

On October 4, 2005, I was transferred to the South Florida Reception Center (S.F.R.C.) in Miami for a dental appointment. While the airplane flew over Miami International Airport, nearby the Lord confirmed my assignment was to reach the lost by teaching and preaching the Gospel. There was a cause and work that needed to be done in the hearts of the men that were passing through S.F.R.C. daily. They were being committed to and oriented in D.O.C. or they were transitioning from one prison to another from Pensacola to Miami (*the entire state of Florida*).

S.F.R.C's environment brings to mind a scene I believe the Apostle Paul was exposed to in a city called Corinth in Greece, where the Corinthian Church was established. Corinth was a major trade route and enjoyed a thriving economy. Sailors and merchants from adjoining nations in the most culturally diverse environments flocked to Corinth with their goods. The City of Corinth was a strategic center of influence for the Gospel of Christ because the travelers who heard the Gospel there could carry it to distant parts of the world.

Similar to, but somewhat different from the City of Corinth, at S.F.R.C., D.O.C. is a thriving big business in which over 100,000 inmates from every ethnic group are incarcerated in over seventy-five prisons throughout the State of Florida.

Moving forward under the leadership of the Holy Spirit, I began to teach Bible studies every morning, Monday through Friday from 9:00 a.m. to 10:30 a.m. on the Rec. Field in front of I-Dorm. I would open with prayer and sing a few songs of Zion as an average of thirty to forty men came daily to fellowship. The subjects taught included basic foundational principals of Christianity such as repentance, faith, forgiveness, the Gospel, the Kingdom of God, and salvation. Even the officers came to hear the Word of God and to ask questions at the Bible studies.

Every Friday from 1:00 p.m. to 2:00 p.m., I preached the Gospel of Christ on the Rec. Field in front of J-Dorm. Men were receiving Christ and their deliverances in leaps and bounds. Signs and wonders including miracles and healings were manifested as the Word went forth. Talvin Thompson from Pilesgrove, New Jersey was one of the many men who repented from his backslidden condition to receive his deliverance under my ministry at S.F.R.C. Upon his release from prison, he moved back to New Jersey and maintained communication with me by mail.

During a telephone conversation with my cousin Michael, he informed me that his mother, Mrs. Atline Cooper, had passed away on March 2, 2006. Mrs. Atline was one of the mothers at Macedonia Church who kept me in line and covered me in prayer. She always addressed me as "Turkey Red" whenever she spoke to me. She always had my best interests at heart, which compelled her to keep the pressure on me to do the right thing before the Lord. The seeds of Mrs. Atline's words of righteousness weren't in vain. Her beloved family and others who knew her, including me, miss her greatly.

Meanwhile, during the six months I was at S.F.R.C. in Miami, I led sixty men to repentance and to receive Jesus Christ as their personal Lord and Savior. Countless men received their deliverances from all sorts of bondages and the backsliders were reclaimed and restored back to a right relationship with God by the power of His Word.

I had completed my dental appointment and Kingdom assignment in Miami, and I was transferred back to Martin C.I. on May 9, 2006. It was at Martin C.I. where I was introduced to one of the KAIROS members named Brad who inspired me to write a book about my life. Brad shared with me that my life was a must-read story. I had never entertained that thought and wasn't very interested in writing my story, but thanks to Brad, I reconsidered.

ENDNOTES

1 "But God demonstrates His own love toward us, in that while we were still sinners, Christ died for us. Much more then, having now been justified by His blood, we shall be saved from wrath through Him. For if when we were enemies we were reconciled to God through the death of His Son, much more, having been reconciled, we shall be saved by His life. And not only *that*, but we also rejoice in God through our Lord Jesus Christ, through whom we have now received the reconciliation."

2 "For God so loved the world that He gave His only begotten Son, that whoever believes in Him should not perish but have everlasting life."

3 "And she will bring forth a Son, and you shall call His name Jesus, for He will save His people from their sins."

4 "The next day John saw Jesus coming toward him, and said, "Behold! The Lamb of God who takes away the sin of the world!"

5 "For as by one man's disobedience many were made sinners, so also by one Man's obedience many will be made righteous."

6 "Jesus answered and said to them, 'You are mistaken, not knowing the Scriptures nor the power of God.'"

7 "And you *He made alive*, who were dead in trespasses and sins."

8 "Therefore, to him who knows to do good and does not do *it*, to him it is sin."

9 "Therefore by the deeds of the law no flesh will be justified in His sight, for by the law *is* the knowledge of sin."

10 "Whoever commits sin also commits lawlessness, and sin is lawlessness."

11 "All unrighteousness is sin, and there is sin not *leading* to death."

12 "If we confess our sins, He is faithful and just to forgive us *our* sins and

to cleanse us from all unrighteousness."

13 "My little children, these things I write to you, so that you may not sin. And if anyone sins, we have an Advocate with the Father, Jesus Christ the righteous."

14 "And He Himself is the propitiation for our sins, and not for ours only but also for the whole world."

15 "He who says, 'I know Him,' and does not keep His commandments, is a liar, and the truth is not in him. But whoever keeps His word, truly the love of God is perfected in him. By this we know that we are in Him. He who says he abides in Him ought himself also to walk just as He walked. Brethren, I write no new commandment to you, but an old commandment which you have had from the beginning. The old commandment is the word which you heard from the beginning. Again, a new commandment I write to you, which thing is true in Him and in you, because the darkness is passing away, and the true light is already shining. He who says he is in the light, and hates his brother, is in darkness until now. He who loves his brother abides in the light, and there is no cause for stumbling in him."

16 "For any kind of trespass, *whether it concerns* an ox, a donkey, a sheep, or clothing, *or* for any kind of lost thing which *another* claims to be his, the cause of both parties shall come before the judges; *and* whomever the judges condemn shall pay double to his neighbor.

17 "You shall neither mistreat a stranger nor oppress him, for you were strangers in the land of Egypt. You shall not afflict any widow or fatherless child."

18 "Therefore let him who thinks he stands take heed lest he fall."

19 "For if anyone thinks himself to be something, when he is nothing, he deceives himself."

20 "I will give you a new heart and put a new spirit within you; I will take the heart of stone out of your flesh and give you a heart of flesh."

21 "And when Jesus went out, He saw a great multitude; and He was moved with compassion for them, and healed their sick."

22 "Now a leper came to Him, imploring Him, kneeling down to Him and saying to Him, 'If You are willing, You can make me clean.' Then Jesus, moved with compassion, stretched out His hand and touched him, and said to him, 'I am willing; be cleansed.' As soon as He had spoken, immediately the leprosy left him, and he was cleansed."

23 And those who passed by blasphemed Him, wagging their heads and saying, 'You who destroy the temple and build it in three days, save Yourself! If You are the Son of God, come down from the cross.' Likewise the chief priests also, mocking with the scribes and elders, said 'He saved others; Himself He cannot save. If He is the King of Israel, let Him now come down from the cross, and we will believe Him.'"

24 "Nor is there salvation in any other, for there is no other name under heaven given among men by which we must be saved."

25 "Destruction and misery are in their ways."

26 " . . . if you confess with your mouth the Lord Jesus and believe in your heart that God has raised Him from the dead, you will be saved."

27 "The Lord is not slack concerning His promise, as some count slackness, but is longsuffering toward us, not willing that any should perish but that all should come to repentance."

28 "For this is good and acceptable in the sight of God our Savior, who desires all men to be saved and to come to the knowledge of the truth. For there is one God and one Mediator between God and men, the Man Christ Jesus, who gave Himself a ransom for all, to be testified in due time."

29 "But He needed to go through Samaria."

30 "So ought not this woman, being a daughter of Abraham, whom Satan has bound—think of it—for eighteen years, be loosed from this bond on the Sabbath?"

31 "how God anointed Jesus of Nazareth with the Holy Spirit and with power, who went about doing good and healing all who were oppressed by the devil, for God was with Him."

32 "and that they may come to their senses and escape the snare of the devil, having been taken captive by him to do his will."

33 "And you shall know the truth, and the truth shall make you free."

34 "Therefore if the Son makes you free, you shall be free indeed."

35 "For when we were still without strength, in due time Christ died for the ungodly."

36 "But God demonstrates His own love toward us, in that while we were still sinners, Christ died for us."

37 "For I delivered to you first of all that which I also received: that Christ died for our sins according to the Scriptures, and that He was buried, and that He rose again the third day according to the Scriptures."

38 "but also for us. It shall be imputed to us who believe in Him who raised up Jesus our Lord from the dead, who was delivered up because of our offenses, and was raised because of our justification."

39 "What then shall we say to these things? If God is for us, who can be against us?"

40 "'If it had not been the Lord who was on our side,' Let Israel now say—'If it had not been the Lord who was on our side, When men rose up against us.'"

41 "Indeed they shall surely assemble, but not because of Me. Whoever assembles against you shall fall for your sake."

42 "No weapon formed against you shall prosper, And every tongue which rises against you in judgment, You shall condemn. This is the heritage of the servants of the LORD, And their righteousness is from Me,' Says the LORD."

43 "Most assuredly, I say to you, he who believes in Me, the works that I do he will do also; and greater works than these he will do, because I go to My Father."

44 "And these signs will follow those who believe: In My name they will case out demons; they will speak with new tongues."

45 "And they went out and preached everywhere, the Lord working with them and confirming the word through the accompanying signs. Amen."

46 "Now when they heard this, they were cut to the heart, and said to Peter and the rest of the apostles, 'Men and brethren, what shall we do?'"

47 "And he brought them out and said, 'Sirs, what must I do to be saved?' So they said, 'Believe on the Lord Jesus Christ, and you will be saved, you and your household.'"

48 "While Peter was still speaking these words, the Holy Spirit fell upon all those who heard the word."

49 "No one can come to Me unless the Father who sent Me draws him; and I will raise him up at the last day."

50 "Then he said to Him, 'If Your Presence does not go with us, do not bring us up from here."

51 "So it was, when the days of feasting had run their course, that Job would send and sanctify them, and he would rise early in the morning and offer burnt offerings according to the number of them all. For Job said, 'It may be that my sons have sinned and cursed God in their hearts.' Thus Job did regularly."

52 "And I also say to you that you are Peter, and on this rock I will build My church, and the gates of Hades shall not prevail against it. And I will give you the keys of the kingdom of heaven, and whatever you bind on earth will be bound in heaven, and whatever you loose on earth will be loosed in heaven. Then He commanded His disciples that they should tell no one that He was Jesus the Christ."

53 "One man of you shall chase a thousand, for the LORD your God is He who fights for you, as He promised you."

54 "Then the seventy returned with joy, saying, 'Lord, even the demons are subject to us in Your name.' And He said to them, 'I saw Satan fall like lightning from heaven. Behold, I give you the authority to trample on serpents and scorpions, and over all the power of the enemy, and nothing shall by any means hurt you. Nevertheless, do not rejoice in this, that the spirits are subject to you, but rather rejoice because your names are written in heaven.'"

55 "And these signs will follow those who believe: In My name they will case out demons; they will speak with new tongues."

56 "And Jesus came and spoke to them, saying, 'All authority has been given to Me in heaven and on earth.'"

57 "that at the name of Jesus every knee should bow, of those in heaven, and of those on earth, and of those under the earth."

58 "And He put all *things* under His feet, and gave Him *to be* head over all *things* to the church."

59 "And He is the head of the body, the church, who is the beginning, the firstborn from the dead, that in all things He may have the preeminence."

60 "Now this man purchased a field with the wages of iniquity; and falling headlong, he burst open in the middle and all his entrails gushed out."

61 "And when they had prayed, the place where they were assembled together was shaken; and they were all filled with the Holy Spirit, and they spoke the word of God with boldness."

62 "And with great power the apostles gave witness to the resurrection of the Lord Jesus. And great grace was upon them all."

63 "Where can I go from Your Spirit? Or where can I flee from Your presence?"

64 "The eyes of the Lord *are* in every place, Keeping watch on the evil and the good."

65 "And there is no creature hidden from His sight, but all things *are* naked and open to the eyes of Him to whom we *must give* account."

Twenty-Four

Set Their Hope in God

UPON ARRIVING BACK at Martin C.I., I was assigned to work in the Classification Department as an orderly. Mr. Cooper was my assigned Classification Officer. He was a die-hard New York Jets fan while I was a serious Miami Dolphins fan. Twice a year there was some competitive and intense trash talking between us during our work breaks. I would hit Mr. Cooper with, "There was a breaking news report that there were some Jets flying from New York that went down in a sea of Dolphins in South Florida. Mr. Cooper would fire back with his New York accent, saying that he couldn't wait because everyone knows that Dolphins can't swim in cold weather and that he was simmering his special sauce for some freshly stewed Dolphins.

Though the Classification Department's job was my primary responsibility, I still taught the EE classes and maintained the order of services in the Chapel. The men who were taught and trained in the EE Ministry were challenged to go out on the Rec. Field for on-the-job training (OJT) to witness for Christ. By experience, I was a hands-on example to the men, taking them out to where the rubber meets the road. In other words, confronting lost souls prayerfully with the Gospel of Christ at Martin C.I. was where witnessing was really making a difference.

Getting out of a comfortable classroom setting to go out and witness for the Kingdom is a very challenging endeavor that is also rewarding and everlasting in nature. One of the most challenging confrontations I dealt with in the EE Ministry was a serious eye opener. When one of the men who was enrolled in the EE Ministry missed too many classes without excuse, I sought him out on the Rec. Field to find out what was going on with him. To my surprise, the inmate explained to me that he stopped coming to class because he was gay, had a crush on me and couldn't stop lusting after me while I taught the class. I thanked him for his honesty and told him that I was totally not interested. I then prayed and bound that unclean spirit in Jesus' name, to shut down the infatuation. [*Galatians 5:19*[1]; *Mark 7:20–23*[2], concerning lasciviousness]

Meanwhile, the Rec. Field Ministry was re-established with a greater anointing upon my life to preach the Gospel of Christ. Once a month, on the Rec. Field, I would invite Spanish speaking brethren to fellowship and have their own feast amongst the inmates.

On November 16, 2006, one of my fellow ministers of the Gospel, David Collins, passed away, at the age of fifty-two, on the Rec. Field as he was working out with weights. He truly loved the Lord and was a solid example of a Christian in word and deed. David's warm spirit and compassion for God's people are missed greatly within the Body of Christ.

During January 2007, Mr. Inman, the Warden of the program, reassigned me to the Medical Department and instructed me to manage a floor crew to wax and maintain all of Martin C.I.'s tile floors. Also, during the same month, the Spirit of the Lord confirmed to me that I was to submit myself under the anointed leadership of Bishop Gerald Green of the Port St. Lucie Worship Center. Bishop Green and I connected in a covenant relationship to advance God's Kingdom together.

On March 19, 2007, Martin C.I. Work Camp was closed down and all the inmates were moved over to the main unit. James Brown, who labored with me at Desoto C.I. from 2000 – 2002, was transferred to Martin C.I. to labor with me before he was released back into society.

The Lord led me to coordinate with the other inmate ministers of the Gospel to oversee a four-day Camp Meeting Revival out on the Rec. Field on April 12 – 15, 2007. From the preaching of God's Word, the conviction of sin and repentance were evident as men's spirits were refreshed and their souls were restored by the Holy Spirit. Twenty-eight men received Christ as their personal Lord and Savior and several men received deliverance.

In June 2007, my daughter Candee graduated from South Fork High School. Though I couldn't be there with her, I celebrated and rejoiced with her in my heart. I wrote letters to inspire her heart to pursue her dreams and goals.

When the 2007 high school football season kicked off in September, I was locked in and listening to the Friday night broadcasts of my son Adam, Jr. and his teammates playing football for the South Fork Bulldogs. Though I couldn't be there in person to support him, I wrote to him weekly to encourage him and to inform him that

I would be tuned in, listening as he played. My proudest moments came when Adam, Jr. ran back three exciting kick-off returns for touchdowns in three different games.

One of the most important Kingdom truths I shared wisely with all of my children was that playing sports, getting an education, and pursuing their dreams are all wonderful endeavors. However, only what we do and accomplish for Jesus will last for eternity, starting with a right relationship with God through Jesus Christ. I shared my truth with all of my children accordingly so that they will set their hope in God and not in people or materialistic things. [*Psalm 78:1–8*]

On June 5, 2008, my youngest daughter, Turquoise (Q), graduated from Martin County High School with high honors after having received a double promotion (*she had been advanced a grade twice in grammar school*). I spoke with Turquoise by phone to express how proud I was of her, celebrated with her with praises and wishes for the very best in furthering her education as she pursued her dreams and goals. Knowing that her dad couldn't be there, it was sweet and thoughtful of Turquoise to send me my invitation to her graduation commencement exercise.

Turquoise's 2008 class motto stated:

> Still round the corner there may wait,
> A new road or a secret gate;
> And though I oft have passed them by,
> A day will come at last when I
> Shall take the hidden paths that run
> West of the moon, East of sun.
>
> —J.R.R. Tolkien

Turquoise went on to enroll in the College of Medicine at the University of Central Florida (UCF), Orlando, to become a medical doctor.

Just a few weeks later on June 29, 2008, my oldest aunt, Mary Ann Glover, passed away. One of my most memorable recollections of Mary Ann was that she took out an insurance policy on me because she could no longer blackmail me. I was informed of the good news that Mary Ann had set her hope in God by accepting Christ in her heart months before she passed away.

A few days after my 44th birthday on 9/11, an outside source in society informed me that Turquoise was pregnant. I was very surprised by the news and called home to confirm that she was indeed pregnant. I spoke with her grandmother and mother, then I encouraged Turquoise that everything was going to be okay.

Meanwhile, during Adam, Jr.'s 2008 high school football season, every team he faced avoided kicking the ball to him. The South Fork Bulldogs finished their best season ever in a semi-final loss to St. Thomas Aquinas of Ft. Lauderdale, Florida.

On Valentine's Day, 2009, I received an unexpected double surprise visitation. I walked into the visiting park not knowing who had come to visit. While there, I first met Mr. Gray whom I had not seen in eighteen years. Mr. Gray was an elderly pillar in the community of Hobe Sound, Florida. After speaking with him briefly, Mr. Gray said, "Your two girls are over there." I walked toward the table and noticed that Candee's face and stomach were fuller than the last time we visited. I knew that Turquoise was pregnant, but I did not know about Candee's pregnancy. However, I was totally elated to see my two beautiful, pregnant princesses as I exchanged hugs and kisses with them.

It was a wonderful visitation as they both double-teamed me lovingly with their anticipated father-daughter conversation. After I reinforced my unconditional love for them and expressed my total support of their pregnancies, they took rapid turns giving me two ears full of their heartfelt feelings toward me.

Mr. Gray, who was sitting next to them with his son Eric, came to my rescue to clarify some things from a father's perspective, which they both respected. When our visitation came to a close, I laid hands on Candee and Turquoises' stomachs and by faith I spoke God's blessings and protection over my grandkids' lives as Israel did in Genesis 48:14–16[3]. Then I embraced Candee and Turquoise and prayed asking and thanking God in advance for His provision and covering over them. I also asked Him to bless them with successful deliveries of my second generation in Jesus' name.

The very next month, March 23, 2009, to be exact, I was playing Scrabble in the dormitory when I looked up at a breaking news report. My Aunt Helen was being interviewed while crying. The news reporter was trying to get an account as to how her innocent son, Willie Gene Thomas, Jr., had been killed in a drive-by shooting. Realizing what had just happened, I went to my room in tears immediately to intercede in prayer for Helen and the family.

The next day Helen called the Chapel at Martin C.I. to explain what happened. After she expressed her pain and hurt, she assured me that Gene had accepted Jesus in his heart and had been active in Church. I encouraged and comforted Helen's heart, assuring her that because

Gene had set his hope in God by accepting Jesus, he is in a better place with the Lord (*2 Corinthians 5:8*[4]).

During one of my visitations, I enjoyed spending time with my uncle Jimmy Glover (*Ski-Bo*), who was also one of Ma Jennie's equalizers. I also enjoyed a few visits from Mr. Albert Cooper and Mrs. Willie Mae Johnson (*Deacon and mother at Macedonia Church*).

On April 1, 2009, Turquoise birthed Jayden Queen, my first grandson. That was one proud moment. Meanwhile at Martin C.I., on May 11, an inmate was stabbed and died on the Rec. Field. Because of this killing, the compound was split in half and the Lord redirected me to preach the Gospel of Christ every Friday on the Rec. Field from 1:00 to 2:30 p.m. Several times afterward on the Rec. Field, a few brethren and I had to touch and agree in prayer to come against demonic forces to prevent them from influencing men to kill one another with knives. [*Joshua 23:10*[5]; *Deuteronomy 32:30*[6]; *Matthew 18:19–20*[7]]

In June 2009 Adam, Jr. graduated from South Fork, Raven graduated from Martin County High, and Leryia graduated from Port St. Lucie High. I celebrated all of them and expressed in cards how proud I was of them for graduating. Though Adam, Jr. had numerous scholarship offers to play Division 1 football, he decided to enlist in the Marine Corps. Raven and Leryia were undecided as to what they wanted to pursue after graduation.

In addition to corresponding with and receiving visits from my children, another proud moment occurred on July 21, 2009, when Candee birthed Marcus Rogers, my second grandson. Marcus's birth was even more special because he was born on the same exact date as Adam, Jr.

Since Charlie and Lois Rozzell had strokes, the EE Ministry was cancelled. They were overseeing the EE Ministry under the leadership of Dr. D. James Kennedy Ministries of Coral Ridge, Ft. Lauderdale, Florida. Meanwhile Assistant Warden, Mr. Inman, reassigned me to work in the kitchen and promoted me to cook and serve the Administration and Staff of officers. Beside having a lot of quality study and relaxation time twelve hours a day in Staff Dining, this job presented some unique challenges.

Once I created a buzz with my flavor in cooking, it was on among the staff of officers. They didn't know that I could burn like that. Sergeants Caesar from East Stuart and Mitchell from Indiantown knew me personally from the streets. Every chance they got, they made it known that I hadn't always been a preacher who knew how to cook good food. The Lord used them to witness to their colleagues and inmates about who Adam really used to be in society as a major drug dealer. I wouldn't say anything while they talked and I acted as though I didn't know what they were talking about. When I would say the old Adam was buried, Caesar and Mitchell would really start talking about the criminal life I used to live.

Caesar would try his best to wake up Turk. He would say, "Y'all don't know him, but I know that Turk is still in there." I would always assure him that Turk had been crucified with Jesus. [*Galations 2:20*[8]] The only thing that stopped Caesar from taking it too far was when I said I was going to tell Mrs. Sophie (*his grandmother*) on him for using foul language. He would then bring Ma Jennie into the conversation because he knew we both had been raised in the church and that Mrs. Sophie and Ma Jennie didn't play.

On my 45th birthday, September 11, 2009, and on Christmas day, Candee, baby Marcus, and Leryia visited me. All of my children began to visit more regularly by themselves because they were eighteen and older. I had to balance my approach in my conversations with my children because they all had different personalities, strengths, and weaknesses. I learned to enjoy their presence and to hear them out as they expressed themselves uniquely. I always ended our visitations with words of wisdom before praying in Jesus' name.

On January 10, 2001, Jamkevia Ford (*Dankie*) passed away. She was my Aunt Mary's youngest daughter. Dankie was full of life and very humorous. She had a unique way of bringing a smile to the faces of everyone she met.

Meanwhile as I worked in Staff Dining, I was harassed sexually by a female who allowed a Jezebel spirit to influence her actions and behavior. Reporting the harassment would have resulted in a quick transfer and her immediate termination. When she rolled up on me and made her move, I fled out of my assigned area, leaving her there as Joseph left Potiphar's wife when she tried to seduce him in Genesis 39:7–12. I wasn't scared, I knew what to do and hadn't forgotten how to get my groove on, but my integrity and the calling upon my life was more precious than a temporary quick thrill. Can I get a witness? At the first opportunity that presented itself I checked and rebuked her, telling her not to try that again. She shamefully agreed.

Because of my Staff Dining job I experienced a serious threat to my life when I was accused falsely of being a snitch. Being labeled a snitch in prison, especially at Martin C.I., is like a signed death warrant for an individual's life. Walking to the most dangerous and worst dorm, the "Dog House," where I lived, I was informed by several inmates that my locker had been broken into. Once inside the dorm I assessed my property and then prayed asking God for His protection and wisdom in addressing a dorm full of thugs who hated what I stood for—Jesus and righteousness. By not confronting the problem immediately, it would have indicated that I was guilty as labeled and a coward for not being willing to stand up for myself as a man, neither of which was true.

With my life on the line as a crowd of about fifty thugs looked on with an intensely demonic atmosphere, thoughts of my children and my future in society flashed through my mind. The Spirit of the Lord assured me within that He wasn't going to allow the enemy to take me out in the Dog House. With that assurance and only by the grace of God, after I unplugged the TV in the day room to confront the source who fabricated the false rumor, the Lord calmed that storm.

Minutes later when word got out on the compound that I had been disrespected and tried, the ZOS (*Haitian gang*), Muslims, Aryan Nation, Latin Kings, and some other angry thugs stepped to me as I walked to the Rec. Field. They wanted me to point out the perpetrators so they could slide (*sneak up on them*) and really give them the business for messing with God's anointed, but I assured them all that God had already fought my battle.

Because of the potential scenario lingering in the air that I may have to defend myself by all means necessary, I informed Sergeant Caesar of my situation in the event that something popped off.

On August 17, 2010, Ernest Attenbury arrived at Martin C.I. He was one of the mentors and fellow ministers of the Gospel who came to labor in the ministry. On May 11, 2011, after witnessing personally the suicide attempts of several young men by hanging or cutting in the confinement dorm, God released a vision in my Spirit for the establishment of a deliverance class at Martin C.I.

The next day Mr. Inman (*Assistant Warden*) came by Staff Dining, where I shared the vision with him and the reason why God said the deliverance class was needed. Mr. Inman asked several questions which I answered as the Lord led me. My responses alleviated his concerns. Mr. Inman then told me to be specific when outlining the purpose, objective, foundation, and mission for the deliverance class in a proposal to the Senior Warden.

The purpose of the deliverance class was to create an atmosphere in which God's anointing was released to destroy yokes and liberate the bound, wounded, and hurting. The objective of the class was to invite whosoever would come to be saved, healed, and delivered. The foundation of the class was Jesus Christ and the Word of God. The mission was to lead the lost to Christ on the authority of God's Word and to administer deliverance to the captive, as well as building and advancing God's Kingdom in the hearts of believers from the inside out with the Word of God.

I was going to be the primary teacher and preacher, ministering from the Gospels of Matthew, Mark, Luke, and John. Other proven and qualified Christian inmates would be imparting the Word of God as well. Approved volunteers would be on hand to oversee and to minister the Word also. I requested four hours from 3:30 to 7:30 p.m. so that we could take advantage of the time through the count time (*roll call*). That is, normally during roll call (*when the officers count the inmates*) all inmates are required to be in the dormitories where they sleep. Therefore, instead of inmates being in the dormitories during count time, some of us would be in the building where the service was conducted. Everything conducted in the Friday Night Deliverance Class (FNDC) would be done decently, in order, and in compliance with security protocol.

On May 23, 2011, the proposal for the deliverance class was approved by Senior and Assistant Wardens, Mr. Reid and Mr. Inman, respectively. On June 3, 2011, Martin C.I.'s Friday Night Deliverance Class was officially established.

Assistant Warden Inman, volunteers Pastor John Odom, Minister Michael Cooper (*ex-convict*), and seventy-six hungry believers were in the house for the first FNDC. The other approved volunteers who pressed their way out to Martin C.I. to fellowship with the men were Bishop Gerald Green, Leroy Masters, Guy Francis, Samori Williams, Pastor Leon Hall, and Michael Poke. The FNDC was the place to be every Friday from 3:30 to 7:30 p.m. for men to have their Spirits quickened and their souls restored and refreshed with the Word of God.

The FNDC ministry took off in a saturated, anointed atmosphere as I established the purpose, objective, foundation, and mission of that ministry. The men were encouraged that they had an important part to play in helping to maintain the anointed atmosphere in the House. In other words, by being in one accord, they invited God's deliverance and healing power into the House. The men were also required to bring their own Bibles because I informed them that book, chapter, and verse would be given for their spiritual growth and development as the messages and teachings went forth. FNDC's praise reports were written down weekly to keep an account of what took place in the classes. I gave the written reports to Mr. Inman personally. I announced to the men that every decision we made concerning FNDC would be based upon the Word of God.

The Lord led me to select a FNDC Board of faithful men to establish accountability among my peers and Kingdom balance in the ministry. The Board was made up of Ernest Atterbury, Derick Thompson (*DT*), Brian Kennedy, Darick Edwards, Feuwshay Walker, Jerry Hemphill, Eddie Humphrey, and Albert Hallmon. All of the men ministered the Word of God as the Spirit of the Lord led me to release them to do so.

Ernest Atterbury and DT were God's second and third generals in command next to me. They were my closest friends and confidants in whom I confided. I valued their spiritual insight and wisdom. I understood that my primary calling involved an evangelistic mantle upon my life, but now the Lord had granted me a greater anointing with the liberty to operate with a pastoral mantle. Therefore, in this ministry, I had to operate and flow with a shepherd's heart to serve with more compassion and wisdom toward the men.

As the FNDC Ministry went forth men's lives were being transformed radically by the Word of God. Men received Christ, hearts were healed, backsliders were restored, many received their deliverance, and demons were cast out of men in Jesus' name. Men came to FNDC with the expectation that they would receive something from the Lord, and they left the class changed men. A few homeboys who witnessed this great move of God had been saved prior to the FNDC, including Calvin Jackson, Elston Powel, and Robert Newman.

Upon Calvin's and Robert's obedience, they were given a few opportunities to proclaim the Word of God. On Easter 2012, the Lord led me to present the Easter Ministry play in the Chapel again to Martin C.I. administration, outside volunteers, and the inmate population.

Pastor John Basham and his wife from Home Sound and Pastor John Odom and his wife with their friends were truly blessed as the men profoundly re-enacted Jesus' ministry, death, burial, and resurrection.

On June 15, 2012, for the FNDC's first year anniversary I baked my favorite, and now, famous dessert for the men on the FNDC ministry team, a sweet mouthwatering upside-down pineapple cake, of which several of the C.Os. also couldn't resist. The cake was served with Dunkin Donuts coffee after they watched the movie *Courageous*.

Upon Bishop Gerald Green and Leroy Master certifying officially that the cake was the real deal, all the men had a wonderful time fellowshipping as they took turns sharing what they learned from the movie. There was a tremendous response from the men as they expressed individually and collectively what they learned concerning becoming men and being held accountable as Godly priests, providers, and protectors of their respective families.

During July, things that were birthed in the Spiritual realm started to manifest and take place in the natural realm. This brought about a shift at Martin C.I. First, Mr. Inman was forced into retirement. Then, Mr. Lawrence, the new Assistant Warden of Programs, advised me personally to restructure the Rec. Field Ministry. He also told me that he totally supported the FNDC in the Chapel. I sensed that my breakthrough and departure from Martin C.I. was drawing near. There was a demand upon my life to do all I could for the Kingdom while I was there. It was critical and wise for me to pass the mantle on to Brother Atterbury as I informed him and DT, with inside Kingdom information, to assume responsibility for the FNDC Ministry.

ENDNOTES

1 "Now the works of the flesh are evident, which are: adultery, fornication, uncleanness, lewdness."

2 "And He said, 'What comes out of a man, that defiles a man. For from within, out of the heart of men, proceed evil thoughts, adulteries, fornications, murders, thefts, covetousness, wickedness, deceit, lewdness, an evil eye, blasphemy, pride, foolishness. All these evil things come from within and defile a man.'"

3 "Then Israel stretched out his right hand and laid *it* on Ephraim's head, who *was* the younger, and his left hand on Manasseh's head, guiding his hands knowingly, for Manasseh *was* the firstborn. And he blessed Joseph, and said: 'God, before whom my fathers Abraham and Isaac walked, The God who has fed me all my life long to this day, The Angel who has redeemed me from all evil, Bless the lads; Let my name be named upon them, And the name of my fathers Abraham and Isaac; And let them grow into a multitude in the midst of the earth.'"

4 "We are confident, yes, well pleased rather to be absent from the body and to be present with the Lord."

5 "One man of you shall chase a thousand, for the LORD your God is He who fights for you, as He promised you."

6 "How could one chase a thousand, And two put ten thousand to flight, Unless their Rock had sold them, And the LORD had surrendered them?"

7 "Again I say to you that if two of you agree on earth concerning anything that they ask, it will be done for them by My Father in heaven. For where two or three are gathered together in My name, I am there in the midst of them."

8 "I have been crucified with Christ; it is no longer I who live, but Christ lives in me; and the life which I now live in the flesh I live by faith in the Son of God, who loved me and gave Himself for me."

Twenty-Five

Res Ipsa Locquitor
(Latin phrase meaning "the thing speaks for itself")

ALL OF A sudden, before my supernatural breakthrough out of prison came to pass, a turn of events began to happen that I can't explain.

On October 19, 2012, writer and reporter Greg Gardener of the Indian River Magazine was assigned by Tallahassee DOC to interview me, Assistant Warden Charles Lawrence, Bishop Gerald Green, and Senior Region Three Chaplain G.S. Collins concerning the Friday Night Deliverance (FND) Ministry.

Before and after my interview with Greg, he experienced the presence and power of God personally in the FND service as Derek Thompson (*D.T.*) and Bishop Green preached an anointed word in the Chapel at Martin C.I.

On November 5, 2012, the 4th District Court of Appeals (D.C.A.), West Palm Beach, Florida, inquired as to the progress of my pending Rule 3.800(*a*) Motion to correct my illegal sentencing by the Circuit Court, Martin County, Florida.

On November 9, 2012, I responded back to the Fourth D.C.A. and on November 30, 2012, they informed me of the proper writ of legal action I had to file in order to receive an immediate response from the Martin County Circuit Court.

On December 12, 2012, I filed a Petition for a Writ of Mandamus in the 4th D.C.A., West Palm Beach, to request that the Circuit Court, Martin County, rule on my pending Rule 3.800(*a*) Motion.

On January 2, 2013, I was totally surprised to be reunited with my favorite uncle, Charles Glover (*Mickey*), whom I hadn't seen in twenty-one years. Mickey arrived at Martin C.I. not knowing what to expect and ran right into his favorite nephew. For us, it was an emotional and exclusive family reunion.

We immediately touched base concerning family and caught up on our lost years. We missed each other and all the crazy adventures we had engaged in together. I was living a Spirit-filled Christian life before Mickey and that was foreign to him. However, he witnessed personally his nephew living for Jesus, and teaching, and preaching the Gospel of Christ.

Mickey began attending all of the Christian services with me that we had at Martin C.I. He also became an usher at the FND Services which involved signing the men in. Through Mickey's faithfulness, he earned and landed a staff barber job, cutting the administration's hair.

On January 4, 2013, the 4th D.C.A., West Palm Beach, ordered the Circuit Court, Martin County to show cause within twenty days as to why Adam Jolly's motion should not be granted.

On January 25, 2013, Circuit Judge William L. Roby, Martin County, issued an "Order Requiring Expedited Supplemental Responsive Pleading" to the State Attorney and me. The State was given ten days to respond, and I was ordered to respond after the State.

On February 1, 2013, the State Attorney responded with a frivolous, meritless smoke screen in a desperate attempt to persuade Judge Roby to deny my Rule 3.800(a) motion. In fact, the State had actually conceded, in its response, that they were wrong, and I was correct in my assertion that my sentence was illegal.

On February 7, 2013, I responded with the relevant facts and controlling case law that governed my case. I also asked for a thirty-year sentence as the relief I was entitled to receive.

On April 4, 2013, after twenty-one years of litigating my legal case Pro Se, God turned Judge Roby's heart according to His Word in Proverbs 21:1.[1] Judge Roby granted my Rule 3.800(a) Motion to correct my illegal sentence of fifty years as a Habitual Felony Offender (H.F.O.) with fifteen years minimum mandatory. Judge Roby stipulated the following in his Order granting my Motion.

The Defendant must be resentenced on all counts in this case.

Correct court costs at the time of resentencing.

A public defender will be appointed to represent the Defendant.

CHAPTER TWENTY-FIVE

The Defendant was sentenced by the Honorable Judge Larry Schack.

The Defendant is entitled to have the original sentencing judge re-sentence him.

The defense counsel must set the resentencing within sixty days.

The defense counsel will provide an Order to transport the Defendant from his place of incarceration to the St. Lucie County Jail, Ft. Pierce, Florida, to await re-sentencing.

Done and ordered in the Chambers, Stuart, Martin County, Florida, on April 4, 2013.

I didn't question why Judge Roby ordered me to be re-sentenced by Judge Schack in Ft. Pierce, which is thirty miles North of Martin County. I guess it was because Judge Schack was the one who sentenced me to the illegal sentence twenty-one years ago when he was in Martin County. More important to me was the fact that Judge Roby granted my Rule 3.800(a) Motion.

He could have ordered me to be re-sentenced on the moon, it really didn't matter. After praising and thanking God for what He had just done in my life, I sensed in my Spirit that the Lord had a purpose for me getting re-sentenced in Ft. Pierce, Florida, where my crime didn't happen.

Though I was excited that my sentence had been adjudicated as illegal and was overturned, I knew that the fight for my freedom wasn't over. This presumption became very clear to me when the Public Defender showed up on April 30, 2013, to see me in the visiting park at Martin C.I. concerning representing me in court.

During our conversation I discerned very quickly by the Spirit of the Lord that this Public Defender had been appointed to spy out my knowledge of the law and that he meant me no earthly good. In other words, this attorney had been appointed to paralyze my legal defense by sabotaging it and seeing to it that I got another illegal sentence of 50 years.

During our conversation I asked him if he had read my granted Motion and what was the State Attorney's position. His exact response was that he couldn't wrap his mind around my granted Rule 3.800(*a*) Motion and that they (*the State Attorney and the Court*) were going to re-sentence me to another fifty-year sentence. He then had the audacity to try and convince me with a play of semantics of words and meritless case law to justify another illegal 50-year sentence.

This Public Defender's deceptive intentions became even more obvious on May 15, 2013, the date I was ordered and scheduled to be in court for re-sentencing. Instead of the court appearance this attorney had arranged for a conference call in which he informed me that he had postponed my resentencing without my consent while I was still in prison at Martin C.I.

That wasn't right because they (*the Public Defender Attorney, the State Attorney, and the Court*) weren't playing fair.

With my back already to the wall, the judicial system against me, and having already experienced rock bottom by going as low as any man could go in my situation, they forced my hand into making my next most critical legal move.

On July 3, 2013, in another conference call at the prison during a Nelson Hearing (*a hearing to determine whether or not I was qualified to represent myself pro se*) with Judge Schack, the State Attorney Patrick Gillen and the Public Defender, I officially fired this attorney for who he really was, Res Ipsa Locquitor (*a Public Pretending Play Lawyer and Sell Out Artist*).

Having never represented myself in court, I found myself in unfamiliar territory. I was somewhat nervous but not intimidated or fearful because God had not given me the Spirit of fear; He had given me His Spirit of love, power, and a sound mind. [*2 Timothy 1:7*]

The only options before me were to either hire a sentencing specialist lawyer or simply to represent myself, Pro Se. While at Martin C.I. I had already surrounded myself with a legal Kingdom team of sharp paralegal-minded men in blue, so I was prepared for my last option if it came to that, I am very thankful unto God for blessing me with this legal Kingdom team of men in blue, Larry Runge, Joseph Morgan, Tobias Rolle, D.T., and Phillip Davis. They helped prepare and equip me thoroughly in every aspect of what I was about to face in the adversarial arena of the courtroom.

Larry researched my case initially and on July 28, 2011, I filed an Amended Rule 3.800(*a*) Motion to correct my illegal sentence, citing the authority of *Hale v. State*, 630 So.2d 521 (*Fla. 1993*), which was the lethal blow that the State Attorney could not defeat, refute, or handle.

The following is how I met the vessel that God chose to start litigating my legal case. In the month of February 2010, while I was at work one day in Staff Dining preparing food for the administrative staff, I fed Inmate Dante Tucker some fried rice I had cooked and was serving that day. Just as Tucker was eating, Lieutenant Dilio walked through the Staff Dining area and had both of us locked up for destroying state food (*serving food to an inmate that had been prepared for administrative staff*). That's what he wrote in the Disciplinary Report (D.R.).

I served eight days in confinement (*jail*) for the only D.R. I had ever received while at Martin C.I. since 1999. In the last two hours I was in confinement before they let me out, I was placed in a cell with a White inmate named Larry Runge. I didn't know who he was, but he knew who I was and where I worked.

When I entered the cell, Larry was fascinated with the fact that the administration had locked up a preacher and their staff cook. Martin C.I. doesn't discriminate against anyone, not even the blind, handicapped, or crazy, and in my case, not even a Christian Preacher who had crossed the line.

For the sake of my conscience and the restoration of my right standing before God, I repented unto the Lord and apologized to my Supervisor, Mr. Harris, and moved on.

Larry was a very distinguished person. He was intelligent, well-educated and was living out his alternative lifestyle as a homosexual. I had an uncle named Ricky who lived a homosexual lifestyle. He lived a short life, so I understood Larry's lifestyle somewhat and didn't look down on him.

For the record, I am not against any person living in homosexuality, but I am against the spirit behind them that promotes the lifestyle, just like the Apostle Paul was against the spirit of divination and not the woman possessed of that spirit. [*Acts 16:16–18*[2]]

Jesus Christ in my Spirit is far greater than what was in Larry, so I felt no pressure being in the same cell with him. What it did give me was a divine appointment to share the love of God with him and to witness Christ to him. I asked him how he knew who I was and where I worked. He replied, "Everyone knows you, Jolly, and I've eaten some of your delicious cooking you brought to my Supervisor, Mrs. Amdol the Librarian.

During our conversation, he mentioned that he had worked for a law firm in Ft. Lauderdale, Florida. I didn't put any stock into his claim, and I wasn't impressed with his eloquent speech and knowledge of the law because everybody in prison has a story to tell and I wasn't going to be Shanghaied (*bamboozled*).

After two hours in the cell with Larry, I was released and restored back to my position as the Staff Dining cook. Two weeks later Larry was released and moved into the same dorm with his partner, Muscle. A month later, Muscle and Larry stepped to me with a deal offering me Larry's legal services in exchange for eating Jolly's cooking. With my supervisor's permission, out of the allotted portion of food I cooked, I stipulated to them both that if they attended Church services and allowed me to tell them about Jesus as Larry worked on my case, we had a deal.

One day early in July 2011, after my prayer and devotional time, I shared with Larry Proverbs 16:3. Then I told him that the legal work he was doing for me was being done for the Glory of God and that his thoughts were going to be established by God to win my case victoriously. The rest was history because days later he discovered *Hale v. State*, 630 So.2d 521 (*Fla. 1993*) and on July 28, 2011, I filed the Amended Rule 3.800(*a*) Motion that was granted on April 4, 2013.

Morgan, Tobias, and D.T. drilled and cross-examined me with applicational principles within the parameters of the law concerning my legal case. We were all limited to books the law in the Law Library at Martin C.I. but their knowledge of the law was more advanced than mine. However, they were uniquely skilled and specialized in different areas of the law, with sharp insights and legal understanding.

They were very direct and stern with regard to the law and had a serious attitude against the judicial system. They also had a pit bull mentality with an aggressive approach.

Morgan was savvy with the law and had a photographic memory of controlling Federal and State Law. He knew the history of the law going all the way back to the Star Chamber Tribunal in 1641, when it was abolished. The term "Star Chamber" refers pejoratively to any secret or closed meeting held by a judicial or executive body, or to a court proceeding that is grossly unfair or that is used to persecute an individual.[3] Morgan also had a proven track record under his belt of representing himself Pro Se with a 3 – 2 win-loss record at trial.

Tobias was very sound and methodical with regard to his research, making sure he was on point with a legal perspective. Tobias schooled me patiently with a few legal courtroom strategies so I could defend myself effectively.

Derek (*D.T.*) was wise spiritually in and with the law, which gave him an edge to discern precisely what law was applicable, or not, in any particular case. D.T. instructed me to not deviate from the four corners of my granted Rule 3.800(*a*) Motion during the re-sentencing proceeding because the courtroom operates in another language and on a different level.

Mr. Phillip Davis happened to be a real-life Circuit Court Judge out of Miami who had broken the law and was transported divinely to Martin C.I. on June 7, 2011. Judge Davis began sitting on and serving as one of my key legal advisors on the Kingdom Team! Judge Davis imparted unto me aspects of courtroom etiquette—pros and cons, dos and don'ts, including when to speak and when not to speak. Most importantly, he taught me that less is more when speaking in the courtroom while representing myself, Pro Se.

I had a serious challenge before me of balancing the valuable information I had gleaned from my legal Kingdom Team. After they dropped on me some serious, insightful, and carefully thought-out advice, I filed two Motions to move the State Attorney to tilt their hand to expose his or their intended course of action. I filed a Motion for a Conflict Free Counsel and a Motion for Discovery.

It was my legal right to file these particular Motions to receive valuable information in order that I may make the most informed decision to win in the Court of Law. It was also a legally prudent and strategic move on my part to establish myself in the best possible position while heading into the most serious fight of my life for my physical freedom.

I filed a Motion for Conflict Free Counsel because, remember, I fired that play, play sell-out artist Public Pretender Attorney. Any time you fire a public defender attorney with a valid reason, the Court is obligated to hire the Defendant a private attorney—that's the law.

I filed the Motion for Discovery to compel the State Attorney to release and turn over to me copies of all of its relevant information, material, evidence, and the names of the Prosecution's witnesses that they planned on using against me in a Court of Law.

On October 21, 2013, by and through the hands of a certified D.O.C. employee, I received the State Attorney's

Discovery Response that included the names of the witnesses and the evidence they planned, with certainty, to use against me.

With the discovery information I was then privy to the State's strategy and position concerning how they were going to attack me with their deceptive legal intent.

The key for me in getting this information was that it allowed me to prepare myself to be ready to execute and strike with precision in Court when appropriate. Something special was happening that was bigger than me and greater than my situation.

I sensed in my Spirit that God was orchestrating things from behind the scenes for His honor and His glory. His Holy Word does say, "And we know that all things work together for good to those who love God, to those who are the called according to His purpose" (*Romans 8:28*).

When I was transported to outside Court, I couldn't help but to be awestruck at the very sight of society, especially while traveling over the new Roosevelt Bridge in Stuart, Florida, because it was one of the places I fished and played under with my brothers and neighborhood friends while growing up. If you served twenty-one-and-a-half years (*more than two decades*) in prison, how do you think you would respond to the sight of society? Don't kid yourself. Think about that.

On October 23, 2014, at 2:00 p.m., I arrived at Ft. Pierce, Florida in Courtroom 1B before Circuit Court Judge Larry Schack, State Attorneys Patrick W. Gillen, Jr., and Rick Seymour. I entered the courtroom in shackles, chained up with leg restraints and handcuffs, which led me to wonder if Moses felt similarly when he appeared before Pharaoh. I was finally before the Judge who sentenced me two decades prior.

Present in the courtroom on my behalf were twenty-two watchful and prayerful character witnesses along with my daughter Candee (*who was seven months pregnant*), my family and friends.

Immediately after the Court preliminaries and before the re-sentencing proceeding started without a lawyer, I moved for the Judge to give me an opportunity to resolve my case with the State Attorney privately.

Judge Schack granted my request for a 30-minute grace period in which to handle our business. He then asked everyone to exit the courtroom while he retreated to his chambers.

Before leaving the courtroom, the Judge informed the State Attorneys and me that our conversation was being recorded. Four serious-looking, armed Courtroom Officers monitored our intense negotiations. We were like Republicans and Democrats, each side standing its ground, not willing to budge or blink.

Though I was proactive when initiating a Common Ground Deal (*trying to convince the State Attorney to give me a straight 30- or 40-year sentence without Habitual Offender* (H.O.) *status*), the State was stuck on offering me forty years as a Habitual Felony Offender (H.F.O.). I countered with a straight forty-year sentence.

A forty-year H.F.O. sentence meant that I would have had to serve another three years in prison, whereas a straight forty-year sentence would have resulted in my immediate release.

Wisely, I kept close to my vest the fact that the Judge had limited discretion according to the law that governed my case. That is, I knew that I could only receive a thirty-year H.F.O. sentence or a twenty-seven-year guideline sentence (*a guideline sentence can only include*

a certain amount of time based on a point system). Res
Ipsa Locquitor.

Having this legal inside information concerning my
situation enabled me to remain patient and not get out of
character when everything seemed to be going against me.
I was swift to hear and slow to speak as I listened to what
the State Attorneys had to say because I understood the
old adage that "loose lips sink ships".

After the thirty-minute negotiations Judge Schack
called everyone back into the Courtroom. My heart was
encouraged when my twenty-two character witnesses,
family and friends entered back into the Courtroom.
Further, I took notice of how the Judge and State
Attorneys acknowledged that I had overwhelming support. When they were all seated, Judge Schack asked, "Are
you all here to support Mr. Jolly?" They all nodded their
heads "yes" in collective agreement. The Judge then asked
the parties if we had come to an agreement to resolve the
case and we both said, "No, Your Honor." The very next
thing I couldn't help but observe, out of the corner of my
eye, was that my daughter, Candee, had lost control of her
emotions. She was in a ball of tears and shaking visibly.
I had to quickly numb her out and refocus my attention
on the fight that I was in because I couldn't afford to get
emotional in the spot I was in.

When the Court proceedings went forward, my spiritual eyes were open to see, and my ears were attentive
to hear. Immediately I sensed a shrewd legal curve ball
that had been thrown my way to jam me up in my Pro Se
representation. I didn't blink, fake pump, or stutter with
my next prepared move.

When the Judge directed me to respond, I did the unexpected and threw my heated legal fast ball, moving for the Judge to postpone and reschedule my sentencing.

Upon my petition the Judge said that I could not postpone this hearing, then I immediately responded with my prepared federal and state controlling laws which afforded me the legal right to do so. After my response, the Judge asked the State Attorneys if they had any objection and they said, "No, Your Honor." Then Judge Schack re-scheduled my re-sentencing for December 4, 2013, at 2:00 p.m. and advised me that we needed to resolve the matter on that date without any further delays. I assured him that we would do so.

Back at Martin C.I. on October 30, 2013, while watching the baseball World Series between the Boston Red Sox and the St. Louis Cardinals, I was surprised to receive an unexpected letter from my oldest daughter, Yashekia (*Wienchie*), who lives in Tampa, Florida. Hearing from her by letter really brought joy to my heart. Since my New York Yankees weren't playing for another world title on the big stage, my daughter's letter took precedence over the World Series. I was really touched to know that she was very much aware of my well-being and present situation in court despite the years we lost due to no contact. It was only by the grace of God that I was blessed to be reconciled with my oldest daughter and restored to a loving father-daughter relationship.

A few days later I received encouraging letters from my two youngest daughters, Raven and Turquoise. They both celebrated with me in advance of my breakthrough in court and expressed their anticipation of my coming home to fulfill my responsibility in their lives as their father.

While my situation at that time was unfolding in court and in my personal life, I witnessed the hand and favor of God move on my behalf as the Lord confirmed His Word in my life. God had decreed in His Word that He would restore the years that the locusts (*the enemy*) had consumed, and that He would turn the hearts of fathers to their children and the hearts of children to their fathers. [*Joel 2:25; Malachi 4:6*]

At Martin C.I., on November 2, 2013, we had our first Malachi Dads Graduation and Celebration. Malachi Dads is a faith-based re-entry program for incarcerated fathers, that selected Martin C.I. as the first prison in the State of Florida to be a positive model for other institutions. The program's primary goal is to turn the fathers' hearts toward their children. [*Malachi 4:6*[4]]

The forty men in blue who graduated had striven diligently once a week for ten months to learn how to become better dads and Godly fathers to their children and grandchildren. The reward for the men who completed the program successfully was that they got to enjoy a beautiful day of celebration with their sons, daughters, and grandchildren out on the Rec. Field at Martin C.I.

The men and I, along with our children and grandchildren, enjoyed the special bonding moment that featured a puppet show, bounce houses, T-shirts, photos, music, refreshments, popcorn, and pizza. The Malachi Dads program created a celebration at Martin C.I. which involved a friendly atmosphere that was welcoming and peaceful. I really enjoyed myself and had an awesome time with one of my grandsons, Marcus. Though I finished tearing what I had left of my ACL in my right knee by running around chasing and playing with Marcus, it was worth it.

The Malachi Dads program celebration was a unique success. Thanks to the Prison Fellowship Field Director Tyrus McCloud, Regional Three Director, Regional Three Chaplain, Martin C.I. administration, and all of the wonderful volunteers who helped make the Malachi Dads' celebration possible.

Sometime later, when I had a chance to speak with Candee over the phone, I asked her why she was crying in court. She responded that she had never seen me in chains, and she couldn't stand to see her daddy like that.

In the days, weeks, and hours leading up to my anticipated court date there were two lawyers interested in potentially taking on my case. One attorney was asking for $15,000.00 and the other was asking for $3,500.00. I decided that my best interests weren't in their hearts, and I was, thus, better off and more thoroughly prepared to represent myself Pro Se. In fact, the most critical part of my case had already been litigated and adjudicated in my favor. I just had to walk it out, see it through and articulate my case in the courtroom, which isn't an easy thing to do. My faith and confidence was in God rather than in myself or in another man because, "With men it is impossible, but not with God; for with God all things are possible" (*Mark 10:27*).

After much prayer and fasting, my court appointment at 2:00 p.m. on December 4, 2013, arrived and I found myself sitting before Judge Larry Schack with three State Attorneys sitting to my right. While my character witnesses and friends looked on, I sat quietly, armed with truth, facts, and the law. My mind was fully prepared to accept the chips wherever they may fall. I felt like I could relate to Shadrach, Meshach, and Abednego, who were thrown into a fiery furnace, with the Son of God [*Jesus Christ*] on my side. [*Daniel 3:12 – 28*] That is, I felt extremely confident that I was coming out of this situation victoriously like the three Hebrew boys who came out of the fiery furnace without a scratch and not smelling like smoke.

Before the re-sentencing started I asked the Judge if I could have one of the handcuffs removed so that I could have some liberty to regulate the information I had pre-pared that was before me. Initially, the officers denied my request," then they took me to a side room, removed one handcuff and placed a taser pad on my right leg, informing me that if I made one false move I would be out.

When the re-sentencing started and as the State pre-sented its case requesting another 50-year sentence, their voices went mute in my ears, and everything seemed to move in a blur of slow motion.

Immediately, I began to pray in the Spirit,

Father, you are the God of Abraham, Isaac, and Jacob. I honor and glorify you Lord God for who you are. I praise and worship you God for how you delivered the children of Israel out of Egypt and how you brought them through the Red Sea with a high and mighty hand on eagles' wings.

God, you brought Joshua and the Israelites through the Jordan River. I am confident that you are going to deliver me out of prison and bring me through the court-room in your divine favor.

You said that you would 'never leave me nor forsake me.' That is your Word.

Today, my adversaries have said 'there is no help for me in you God.' You are my helper; I will not fear what man can do unto me. You told Moses, Jehoshaphat, and your people to fear not, to stand Still and See the Salvation of the Lord,' because 'the battle is not yours, but God's'. [*Exodus 14:13 – 14; 2 Chronicles 20:15, 17*]

God, I acknowledge that this battle in the courtroom is not mine, but yours, so I am going to stand still and speak boldly only as you lead me by your Spirit and see the salvation (*deliverance*) of the Lord on my behalf. [Matthew 10:18 – 20[5]] You are my refuge, my strength, and my very present help in this courtroom. No weapon formed against me this day shall prosper.

God, lift up a standard against the State Attorney's attack that has come in like a flood against me. Because my heart is a little overwhelmed, lead me to the Rock that is higher than I.

This re-sentencing, my life and my destiny are in your hands. I need you to show up right here and right now to manifest your power. This is my season and my time to receive my supernatural breakthrough. I am thanking you in advance for what you are about to do because I know that you're a way maker, a mountain mover, and a miracle worker. I am your faithful servant and general in your Kingdom. You said that signs and wonders shall follow them that believe. [*Mark 16:17*] Confirm your Word for your honor and for your glory.

Not my will but your will be done. In Jesus' name I pray. Amen.

The State presented its case and witnesses, assassinating my character in the process. The State Attorneys underestimated my ability to represent myself as

I objected wisely to evidence that was irrelevant and cross-examined one of the State's witnesses.

Upon Judge Schack's instruction and direction I presented my case with my character witnesses. The State Attorneys didn't object to any of my evidence, but the Judge and the State cross-examined my witnesses thoroughly. My witnesses included Pastor Steven Pennell, Classification Officer Dwight Cooper, Pastor Leon Hall, Reverend Woodrow Jackson, Minister Leroy Masters, and Mrs. Edy Hooper.

After being sworn in under oath, each witness stood in the paint and hit it out of the park, like Barry Bonds, on the witness stand. It was really good stuff as my KAIROS Ministry family would say.

The courtroom atmosphere was really saturated with the awesome presence of God's anointing. If you were there you would have thought you were in a church service with Judge Schack in the house. There were even a few "Amens!" shouted out from the Amen Corner of the courtroom audience. I couldn't see who shouted "Amen!" a few times but knowing Mrs. Hooper as I did, I could tell it was probably her. She was one of my character witnesses whom I didn't call upon, so I presumed it was her way of showing her genuine support by expressing her agreement with the truth of my character as Woodrow testified.

The last most critical stage of the re-sentencing proceeding came when both sides had to present relevant evidence to determine the appropriate sentence I was to receive. The State presented its weak evidence first, with no cited authority to support their request that the Judge re-sentence me to another illegal sentence of fifty years. Then with boldness in the face of all odds, I presented relevant evidence anew with legal authority to support the sentence I was entitled to receive.

Afterward, I handed the Judge and State Attorneys copies of my sentence memorandum and copies of my single criminal episode chart. I proceeded further to give them the business as I reiterated my illegal sentence structure skillfully and clearly. I went on to explain how and why the initial sentence was illegal. I then petitioned the Judge to sentence me to 30 years H.F.O. on all counts 1–12 with a 3-year mandatory minimum according to Florida State Statutes 893.13(1)(e)(1) and 775.082(3)(6) (1991), and on the authority of *Hale v. State*, 630 So.2d 521 (Fla. 1993) and *Teague v. State*, 871 So.2d 301 (Fla. 2004), which controlled my case.

Next, I handed the Judge all of my certifications of accomplishment since I had been in prison. In my conclusion, I asked Judge Schack to run all of my sentences concurrently to reflect a thirty 30-year H.F.O. sentence with a three 3-year mandatory minimum with my time served plus all my gain time.

Lastly, I apologized to the Judge, the State Attorney, and my family for my past unacceptable criminal behavior. I also expressed that I had already been punished severely enough by serving 21 years and 10 months and that I had learned my lesson. I concluded by saying, "I now ask this Court to sentence me according to the law that governs my case. Thank you."

Judge Schack then informed the courtroom that he was going into his chambers with all of the information and evidence that had been gathered to determine the appropriate sentence I was to receive.

When the officers of the Court took me back into the holding cell, all of my witnesses and friends went out into the hallway to pray. After 30 minutes of deliberation, the Judge had everyone moved back into the Courtroom. Judge Schack's first words were, "In the 24 years as a Circuit Court Judge, I have never experienced a situation like this one." Then he went on to pronounce the sentence as follows:

The Defendant has appeared in open Court Pro Se. Assistant State Attorney Patrick Gillen was present. The Defendant was adjudicated guilty and re-sentenced as a Habitual Offender on Counts 1, 3, 5, 9, and 11 – 30 years DOC with credit time served 445 days plus all credit from 4/23/1993, with a mandatory minimum of 3 years.

As to Counts 2, 4, 6, 10 and 12 – 5 years DOC with credit time served, 445 plus all credit from 4/23/1993. ALL COUNTS CONCURRENT.

The Court deleted the habitual felony offender provision on Counts 2, 4, 6, 10, and 12.

For clarity, Mr. Jolly's sentence is one 30-year sentence as a habitual felony offender with one, 3-year minimum mandatory with all credit time served.

Upon hearing my corrected sentence pronounced, I found myself releasing uncontrollable tears of joy and praising God for the victory because this breakthrough meant my immediate release from prison. Through teary eyes and unexplainable emotions, I looked over to see my witnesses and friends rejoicing in the Lord for what God had just done for His glory.

After 21 years, 10 months, 4 days and 17 hours, the fight for my freedom was finally over. God not only hastened over His Words to perform and confirm them,

He manifested a miracle and His power for witnesses to behold. He made me a wonder before their very eyes!

God didn't allow the weapons formed against me in the Courtroom to prosper and didn't allow my adversaries to rejoice over me. My Lord God, Jesus Christ was truly my lawyer in that Ft. Pierce, Florida Courtroom from 2:00 to 5:00 p.m. on December 4, 2013. He showed up strong and mighty on my behalf and proved Himself to be my deliverer and my Lord God Jehovah. [*Exodus 6:2–3*[6]]

He was my provider, Jehovah Jireh, [*Genesis 22:8,14*]; He was my battle fighter, Jehovah Nissi, [*Exodus 17:8–16*]; He was my present help, Jehovah Sammah, [*Psalm 46:1*] and He was my peace, Jehovah Shamlon [*Judges 6:23–24*].

For the next twenty-four hours I couldn't stop shedding tears of joy. I got very little sleep the next three days. When I arrived back at Martin C.I., the staff and the men in blue were excited and very happy for me when they heard that I was awaiting immediate release. For the record, not everyone was feeling my breakthrough. The haters and the shovel diggers made known their true, evil feelings and their dislike for me. I felt no pressure because they knew that I was one of God's chosen and anointed generals. My character and consistent daily living for Jesus over the years spoke for itself in the danger zone at Martin C.I.

ENDNOTES

1 "The king's heart is in the hand of the LORD, Like the rivers of water; He turns it wherever He wishes."

2 "Now it happened, as we went to prayer, that a certain slave girl possessed with a spirit of divination met us, who brought her masters much profit by fortune-telling. This girl followed Paul and us, and cried out, saying, 'These men are the servants of the Most High God, who proclaim to us the way of salvation.' And this she did for many days. But Paul, greatly annoyed, turned and said to the spirit, 'I command you in the name of Jesus Christ to come out of her.' And he came out that very hour."

3 quote taken from the First Amendment Encyclopedia referenced online at 'mtsu.edu.

4 "And he will turn The hearts of the fathers to the children, And the hearts of the children to their fathers, Lest I come and strike the earth with a curse."

5 "You will be brought before governors and kings for My sake, as a testimony to them and to the Gentiles. But when they deliver you up, do not worry about how or what you should speak. For it will be given to you in that hour what you should speak; for it is not you who speak, but the Spirit of your Father who speaks in you."

6 "And God spoke to Moses and said to him: 'I am the LORD. I appeared to Abraham, to Isaac, and to Jacob, as God Almighty, but by My name LORD I was not known to them."

Epilogue

I HAD TO rebuke one of Satan's messengers who tried to plant seeds of doubt and discouragement in my Spirit by talking about what God wasn't going to do in my life. The Devil is a liar!

I announced boldly to that messenger of Satan that he and his daddy, the Devil, can't curse what God has blessed. Returning to Martin C.I. briefly gave me an opportunity to witness to the men in blue and plant the seed of hope in their hearts, letting them know that God is still in the salvation and deliverance business.

He did it for me and He can do it for them because He is no respecter of persons. [*Romans 2:11*] Meanwhile because of the well-planned prison escape by two inmates from Franklin C.I., North Florida in October 2013, the DOC didn't want my case to possibly become another Chief Judge Belvin Perry situation (*Judge Belvin was blamed for releasing two inmates that had falsified paperwork with his name on it. Thus, he had signed off on an illegal release, albeit unwittingly*). Therefore, I had to wait for Tallahassee DOC's final approval before I was released from Martin C.I.

While awaiting my clearance from Tallahassee, I spent quality time with my Uncle Mickey, Derick Thompson,

Ernest Atterbury, Calvin Jackson, Robert Newman and Darick Edwards.

Fellowshipping with the rest of the Body of Christ during my last services at Martin County C.I. meant a lot to me. The brethren conducted a service of appreciation for me before I departed which was very special, with a lot of love and tears. Most importantly, the Body of Christ prayed with me and decreed God's provision for me.

As I anticipated my immediate release patiently, I received the news from Candee that she had birthed a healthy Taylor George into this world on January 13, 2014, weighing in at 8 lbs. 7 oz. King George was the fifth grandchild to be added to Jollymania.

Just as I was contemplating how I was going to enjoy spending quality time with my children and grandson, on January 17, 2014, I received the Order and paperwork concerning my sentence and judgment from Judge Schack that authorized and commanded Tallahassee and the DOC to release Ma Jennie's boy, Adam Jolly, immediately.

On February 13, 2014, I experienced my supernatural release back into society. My daughter Candee and new grandson, Taylor George, came to pick me up.

ACCOMPLISHMENTS SINCE MY RELEASE FROM PRISON

- Founder and President of Fisher's of Men kingdom outreach Ministry July of 2014
- Married Ingrid Queen-Jolly May 29th 2015
- Ordained licensed minister of the Gospel of Jesus Christ June 17th 2017
- Received Associate of Ministry March 27th 2018 Jacksonville Theological Seminary JTS
- Received Bachelor of Ministry May 26th 2019 JTS
- Ordained Pastor December 1st 2019 Port St.Lucie International Worship Center
- Launched Bread From Heaven Ministries Stuart,Florida January 4th 2020
- Started Jolly Time Enterprise Pressure Cleaning February 2020
- Received Master of Ministry in Christian Counseling May 24th 2020 JTS
- Received Doctorate of Ministry May 13th 2021 JTS
- Successfully completed Eight years of state probation January 26th 2022

Printed in the USA
CPSIA information can be obtained
at www.ICGtesting.com
CBHW072029240224
4551CB00001BB/1